The Grateful Dead

THE
GRATEFUL
DEAD

The History
of a Folk Story

GORDON HALL GEROULD

Introduction by Norm Cohen

University of Illinois Press

Urbana and Chicago

First Illinois paperback edition, 2000
Introduction © 2000 by the Board of Trustees of the
University of Illinois
Manufactured in the United States of America
⊗ This book is printed on acid-free paper.

Library of Congress Cataloging-in-Publication Data
Gerould, Gordon Hall, 1877–
The grateful dead : the history of a folk story /
Gordon Hall Gerould ; introduction by Norm Cohen.
p.   cm.
Originally published: London: D. Nutt, 1908.
Includes bibliographical references.
ISBN 0-252-02575-X (cloth : alk. paper) —
ISBN 0-252-06882-3 (paper : alk. paper)
1. Grateful dead (Tale)
GR75.G6G3   2000
398.22—dc21   99-047567

1 2 3 4 5 C P 5 4 3 2 1

CONTENTS

INTRODUCTION

Norm Cohen

IT is ironic that "Grateful Dead" more likely evokes images of a popular rock band than of the once widely known folktale from which the musical group took its name.[1] The expression has become so associated with the rock band that when a recent collection entitled *Grateful Dead Folktales* was published, its title page had to bear a note that "*Grateful Dead* is a registered service mark of Grateful Dead Productions and is used with permission. [The publisher] is not affiliated with Grateful Dead Productions."[2]

Gordon Hall Gerould, the scholar who first popularized (if not originated) the English phrase "grateful dead," has long since lost claim to the name in both the public's memory and the machinery of our legal system. This republication of his pioneering study of a worldwide folktale cannot alter any legal minutiae, but it can restore his forgotten scholarship.[3]

Who was Gordon Gerould? Who, if not a rock group, were the "grateful dead"? The epithet refers to a character in a number of folktales who, typically, has died penniless (or has committed some other sin) and consequently is left unburied. The hero, a young lad on a quest, volunteers his last cent to see that the corpse receives proper burial. Continuing on his journey, the hero meets a stranger who offers to accompany him and assist him in his quest, whatever it may be. In the end of the tale, we learn that the stranger is the ghost or spirit of the dead man, repaying the hero for his good deed. If this simple story had sur-

vived for two millennia without alterations, folktale scholars
could deal with it rather summarily. As it happens, however, in
that long time span, the theme borrowed from and mixed with
many other common tale motifs, and a study unraveling its variations was needed. Gerould provided the first systematic study
of the theme.

Gerould was born in Goffstown, New Hampshire, on 4
October 1877, the son of the Reverend Samuel Lankton Gerould and Laura Etta (Thayer) Gerould. He was graduated from
Dartmouth in 1899 with a B.A. and received a B. Litt. from
Oxford in 1901. His next five years were spent as a reader in
English on the faculty of Bryn Mawr, where he met his future
wife. In 1905, he joined the Princeton faculty as one of a group
of forty-seven preceptors invited by Princeton's president, Wood-
row Wilson, to inaugurate his new method of instruction: "Our
object," Wilson explained, "has been to take our instruction as
much as possible out of the formal classrooms and get it into the
lives of the undergraduates, depending less on lectures and written tests and more on personal conference and intimate counsel."[4] Gerould advanced to full professorship in 1916. In 1918, his
teaching career was interrupted for a year when he served as
captain in the U.S. Army. (In his file, there is a letter written to
Professor V. L. "Wilkie" Collins at Princeton asking if he knew
any Princeton graduates who might volunteer for the Trench
Warfare Section of the Ordnance Department—"men of the
highest possible capacity and attainments to gather information
in France and England and bring it to us here [in Washing-
ton]."[5] He was appointed to the Advisory Committee of the
College League for Al Smith for President in 1928. In 1938, he
was named incumbent of the Holmes Professorship of Belles
Lettres, Princeton's oldest endowed chair. He became chairman
of the English Department in 1942, a post he held until he
retired in 1946. Though for many years he supervised his department's Committee on Graduate Study, he never took a doctor-
ate himself. Nonetheless, Gerould was a leading authority on
fiction, medieval literature, and folklore, serving as president of

the Medieval Academy of America and vice president of the Modern Language Association. His book-length publications included *The North-English Homily Collection* (1902), *Sir Guy of Warwick* (1905), *Selected Essays of Fielding* (1905), *Saints' Legends* (1916), *The Legend of St. Wulfhad and St. Ruffin at Stone Priory* (1917), *Poems of James Thomson* (1927), *Old English and Medieval Literature* (1929), *Sixteenth Century Literature* (1929), *Beowulf and Sir Gawain and the Green Knight* (1929), *The Ballad of Tradition* (1932), *How to Read Fiction* (1937), *The Patterns of English and American Fiction: A History* (1942), and *Chaucerian Essays* (1952). He also wrote four novels: *Peter Sanders, Retired* (1917), *Youth in Harley* (1920), *Filibuster* (1924), and *A Midsummer Mystery* (1925). Three of his five siblings were also distinguished academics: James Thayer Gerould was librarian of Princeton University and the author of numerous publications; John Hiram Gerould was a professor of biology at Dartmouth; and Harriet Dupee Gerould served on the faculty of Wellesley and as dean of women. Gerould's wife, Katharine Fullerton Gerould, was also a very successful novelist, essayist, and teacher.

Gerould's last years were spent in Asheville, North Carolina, where his daughter lived. He died on 10 April 1953. Upon his death, his former colleagues on the Princeton faculty wrote:

> Whatever his activity as teacher or scholar, Gordon Gerould sought always the qualitative best. His fine sense of literary and ethical values led him to fashion a view of books and people wherein criticism and grace were happily blended. His critical irony could vary from the precision of steel to the genial play of a delicate humor, but never the one without the possibility of the other. In a wider sense, the author, the scholar-critic, and the man were closely intermingled in the sort of character which has always been the glory of English men of letters and which has become so rare in our time. His essential modesty, his unfailing kindness, his behavior under conditions of adversity, all provided evidence that in the end it was the grace rather than the criticism which won out with Gordon Gerould.[6]

To folklorists, who have best honored his memory, Gerould has been remembered primarily for two publications: *The Ballad of Tradition* and *The Grateful Dead: The History of a Folk Story*. *The Ballad of Tradition* was for several decades a high-water mark in ballad scholarship in the English language.

In the nineteenth century, interest in ballads reached a climax with the publication of Francis James Child's monumental work, *The English and Scottish Popular Ballads*, a compendium of every trace of English-language ballads that Child, Harvard's eminent authority on medieval literature, could find in print, manuscript, or living tradition.[7] Unfortunately, Child died before he could write a proper introduction to the subject, so the world was left without his answer to several questions that plagued all those whose interests crossed his: what is a ballad? who wrote them? how does one characterize them? Into the void stepped Child's follower, Francis Gummere, with his 1907 book, *The Popular Ballad*, an influential work championing the argument that ballads were anonymous not because of authors' carelessness or modesty but because they had no single author, being more or less collectively written by the community whence they sprang. This position was attacked and defended for over a decade, mostly by American scholars who were invigorated by the discovery in the first decades of the century that the ballad corpus was not a closed book; ballads were still widely sung in communities throughout the eastern United States and the British Isles.[8] This revelation—at least its magnitude—would probably have stunned Child had he lived to see it. He sought out ballads in living tradition, but his efforts were met with very limited returns; so far as he knew, ballad making and singing were moribund, if not dead, customs. The discovery of the living tradition gave scholars and collectors, such as Louise Pound in Nebraska and Phillips Barry in New England, fresh insight into the role of ballads in a singing community and helped them formulate ballad concepts that could extend beyond the corpus that Child had so ably delimited. Gummere, for all his erudition, was not a collector, and, like Child, he viewed ballads as creations of the long-gone past. Gummere's position came to be known as the theory of communal composition; its attackers were the individualists, who could not understand how a peasant community of semiliterates could create, in Gerould's words, "the magic that ballad lovers have felt since the days of Philip Sidney."[9]

Onto this still smoldering battlefield of ballad scholarship Gerould marched resolutely with his 1923 article entitled "The Making of Ballads." He argued that the existence of numerous variants of ballads, all of equal artistry, rendered untenable the position that some individual poet had written a ballad that then passed from mouth to mouth by a process that could lead only to detrimental changes, if any. "I fail to see how it is possible to escape the conclusion that in certain regions, long before the beginning of popular education, there developed a tradition of poetic utterance that enhanced the powers common to most illiterate folk and made an extraordinary number of persons capable of putting into noble form such tales as they chose to sing," he declared.[10] In effect, Gerould tried to move the focus away from the origins of ballads to the means by which they were propagated: "the proof of authenticity is . . . the fact that the poem has submitted to processes of molding under the influence of a definite tradition of music and verse-making. . . ."[11] Gerould had long before demonstrated that Child's cannon should not be closed and sealed in his article arguing that "The Bitter Withy" was a ballad fully worthy of inclusion in the corpus, which, had Child known about it, he surely would have incorporated.[12] Now Gerould boldly extended the universe of ballads (at least as defined by the telescopes of the academics) to the nineteenth century in the United States by daring to mention the ballad "John Hardy" of West Virginia in the same breath as the ballads of Child's collection. Gerould's arguments were in general well received, save for a politely hostile attack by Louise Pound, who dismissed much of his thesis with the judgment that what was valid was certainly not new: "Professor Gerould has gone a long way around to arrive at something that most scholars who are not arm-chair theorists but practical collectors would have conceded without discussion."[13] If Pound seethed beneath her respectful prose, she had good cause: eight years earlier, Gerould had reviewed her *Poetic Origins and the Ballad* with an acerbity that fairly pounded on the gates of incivility: "It is a little difficult to know what to say about a book on an important subject when the author of it has given much time and trouble to study and yet is obviously incapable of orderly thought. The industry deserves commendation; but the results are practically worthless and deserve no praise."[14]

Gerould's interest in ballad and song writing was not confined to the classic ballads. One of his first publications featured an interview with Walter Kittredge, author of "Tenting on the Old Camp Ground," "one of the enduring legacies of the Civil War to America."[15] Gerould traced Kittredge's childhood and later years, noting the impact that his compositions had on the public. It also focused his attention on such questions as what makes a song popular—matters to which he would return in his studies of balladry.

Undaunted by the outcries of the wounded Louise Pound, Gerould expanded his arguments on ballad making in *The Ballad of Tradition,* published in 1932. The book was warmly received—in both the popular and the scholarly press. The *New York Times* reviewer wrote, "[It] achieves that seldom-attained double objective: it is a book for both the scholar and the layman. And in all the range of English literature there is no other subject so perpetually interesting and so perpetually teasing as that of the Border minstrelsy which seems not to have been born, but most luxuriantly to have grown."[16] Reed Smith, South Carolina's distinguished ballad scholar, praised the work from start to finish: "Professor Gerould's approach to the ballad field is not only sound and illuminating in general, but is particularly so in regard to this matter of the influence of recent collections and the necessity of taking into account tunes as well as texts."[17] Smith thought Gerould's proposed definition of a ballad as "a folk-song that tells a story with stress on the crucial situation, tells it by letting the action unfold itself in event and speech, and tells it objectively with little intrusion of personal bias" was an improvement over earlier definitions by Gummere and George Lyman Kittredge, and he was particularly impressed by Gerould's cogent analysis of the nature of ballad variation.[18] Gerould's definition continues to be serviceable—provided we recognize that it describes only one of several types of balladry found in the Anglo-American tradition. Gerould's study was reprinted in paperback edition twenty-five years after its initial publication, just four years after his death. It was still the best summary available.

By the time Gerould had turned to balladry as a major pre-occupation, he had already established more than a foothold in the field of medieval studies. In 1916, his *Saints' Legends* joined Gummere's *Popular Ballad* and other volumes in Houghton Mifflin's series The Types of English Literature. In it, he examined the voluminous medieval literature of saints' hagiographies, analyzing with skill the interplay between oral and written history and explaining the persistence of oral history—a phenomenon difficult for the twentieth-century mind to comprehend.

We must move backward another decade to the book that is our major interest: *The Grateful Dead: The History of a Folk Story*, first published in 1908 by David Nutt, London, for the Folk-Lore Society. In this volume, Gerould for a second time tackled a collection of stories and endeavored to establish a familial and chronological relationship among its members. His earlier effort concerned the Eustace Legend,[19] and it is worth quoting its introduction because there he laid out many of the principles that governed his Grateful Dead study. "In any study which involves the consideration of a network of stories, it is chiefly necessary to regard the skeleton upon which the tales in question are build up," he began. While individual incidents are easily changed, the skeleton is not. This "story-skeleton is made up of motive and purpose." The *purpose* "of a narrative is its external intent, whether it be told for religious and moral instruction. . . . whether to raise the boisterous laugh . . . or whether for the pleasure of hearing the exploits of love, war, and adventure. . . ."

The *motive* "is the essential part of a story and survives change of purpose as well as loss of incident." "If the same purpose and motive are found unchanged in two narratives, it is safe to regard them as either analogous or the one as derivative of the other." From these postulates, Gerould moved on to discuss the factors that must be considered in studying the group of stories: "first and foremost, the motive, since narratives which are good enough to live are not invertebrate things; secondly, the purpose, easily changed but important; thirdly, matters of chronology and geography, which are sometimes of the utmost value in determining the relationship of allied versions; and lastly, those tricks of thought and language which occasionally furnish suggestive clues to the mystery of literary borrowing."[20]

With his third factor, Gerould placed his study squarely in the tradition of the historic-geographic method of comparative analysis, though without referring to it by name. This method is sometimes called the Finnish method after its originators, father and son Julius and Kaarle Krohn, who, respectively, applied it to the songs of the Finnish epic, the *Kalevala,* and to the investigation of folktale diffusion. The application to folktales was further codified by Antti Aarne's *Leitfaden der vergleichenden Märchenforschung* (Guide to comparative folktale study) in 1913. These studies were motivated by the successes of linguists in analyzing the diffusion and evolution of the Indo-European languages by using both geographic and chronological evidence for positing the original form of the proto-Indo-European language. Following this methodology, Gerould assembled 108 variants of Grateful Dead tales and proceeded to analyze their content, giving due consideration to historical and geographic variation (to the extent that the information was available to him) to arrive at the origins of the tale and its probable evolution.

For the reader who finds his deft juggling of 108 interrelated stories too fast for the eye to follow, I have included a table at the end of this introduction that lists the tales in the order of Gerould's bibliography, which is also the order in which he discusses them. The table also identifies their salient characteristics as Gerould determined them. (Gerould's order is not random but follows a general geographic trend: he starts with tales from the Middle East or Mediterranean, moves to the Slavic countries, then to the Latin and Iberian sources, then to the Germanic region, ending with versions from England. Irish and Gaelic are included with those from Iberia rather than England.) I have added where the tale was found—if Gerould's identification does not make that obvious—and the earliest date Gerould cites for it, generally a publication date but sometimes an approximate date of a manuscript.[21]

Gerould dealt with many problems of folktale scholarship, not all of which were readily solvable. The first and foremost problem, as anyone who has read many folktales recognizes, is that themes recur in different combinations and in different basic tales. Any substantial corpus of folktales cannot be sorted neatly into discrete piles; it consists of interlinked chains of themes, events, characters, motives, and descriptions. Many of these features readily cross linguistic and cultural boundaries. When can we be sure of consanguinity? When must we settle for polygenesis? Gerould's two earliest tales are both important in tracing origins, yet each poses unique problems.

Another problem is revealed by scanning the column of the table headed "Grateful Dead." It appears that nine tales actually lacked the explicit appearance of the grateful deceased. Yet Gerould concluded, on the basis of other characteristics, that those tales are fundamentally Grateful Dead tales that, in the course of oral transmission, lost the overt appearance of the grateful dead character per se.

This peculiarity of identifying a tale as a particular type in spite of the absence of the primary characteristic of that type occurs elsewhere. A particularly problematic theme is what Gerould called the "Lady and the Monster" theme, which he identified as a variant of the "Water of Life" theme. In footnote 1 on page 126, Gerould identifies this theme as "the story of the woman, who through enchantment or her own bad taste is the mistress of an ogre or some other monster." Later Gerould suggests that all of the Poison Maiden tales have this trait (his Class II on page 149), that the Lady and the Monster theme is akin to the Water of Life theme (see page 127 and elsewhere), and that when the Lady and the Monster theme appears in combination with the Poison Maiden theme, it is quite different from its usual form (see page 126). When themes or motifs are so variable, there is a nontrivial degree of subjectivity in classifying tales as having one theme or another. Gerould is unquestionably as good a guide as any through this classification thicket, but the reader must recognize that other analyses are conceivable.

Gerould indicated some uncertainty whether his oldest tale, the one labeled "Simonides," was really related to the general family. This brief fragment is preserved in Cicero's *De Divinatione.* Since Gerould provides only the Latin text of this anecdote,[22] I quote from an English translation: "And who, pray, can make light of the two following dreams which are so often recounted by Stoic writers? The first one is about Simonides, who once saw the dead body of some unknown man lying exposed and buried it. Later, when he had it in mind to go on board a ship he was warned in a vision by the person whom he had given burial not to do so and that if he did he would perish in a shipwreck. Therefore he turned back and all the others who sailed were lost."[23]

Simonides was a Greek lyric poet, born in 556 B.C.E.; if the anecdote really originated with him, it is over two centuries older than the next of Gerould's versions, the one from *Tobit.* Association with the Stoics does not help pin down a date because the Stoics held forth for several centuries—from the third century B.C.E. to the first century C.E. At the very least, though, it dates to Cicero's day, the first century B.C.E. If one does discount this version, however, there is nothing stronger than conjecture to assert that the Grateful Dead theme originated by itself and then was combined with the other themes. As Gerould argued, "Surely it is more reasonable to believe in the existence of such a parent form than to suppose that an originally complicated form was hacked and hewn asunder to produce new compounds."[24]

Another serious problem was adumbrated in Gerould's concluding chapter:

> It has been shown once again that the story has an organic life of its own. . . . Once started, it will go its way through divers lands and ages, yet retain unaltered the essential features of its plot. Call it story-skeleton, or better, living organism, it always keeps its structural integrity. . . . Of no less importance than this is the fact that whatever serious changes take place in its form are not fortuitous, mere whimsical alterations due to the fancy of story-tellers, but are due to capabilities of expansion or combination in the plot itself.[25]

In other words, Gerould dismissed as inconsequential the role of the story-teller in the evolution of the tale. The teller is merely a passive agent; the tale itself is the living thing. This assumption is necessary if one is to study the tale versions without considering their social context. Gerould anticipated one of the major criticisms leveled at the historic-geographic method: its disregard for the bearers of the tradition. The approach may have worked in the study of linguistics, but tales and ballads are not the culturally neutral artifacts that words are, and what may be valid in linguistic studies need not be in the case of folktales. The questionable validity of this theoretical posture throws comparative analysis into a quandary. Tales or songs or ballads collected in the recent past from oral tradition may function quite differently from their analogs in remote times and places.

The passage of nine decades has not tarnished the glow of Gerould's analyses. However, new tools and resources might have simplified his task had they been available in 1908. For example, Gerould separates his tales into clusters, according to what if any major theme accompanies the Grateful Dead theme itself. His important adjunct themes are "the poison maiden," "the ransomed woman," "the water of life," "the spendthrift knight," "the thankful beast," "the skillful companions, "the two friends," and the "division (or sacrifice) of children." Modern folktale scholarship has two important tools to use in analysis: the notion of tale-type and the notion of motif. Tale-types are the broad-brush plot essences of the tales.[26] Motifs are the traditional unitary building blocks out of which tales are constructed.[27] Both have been catalogued extensively for different cultures. With the vantage point of these resources, we see that some of Gerould's themes are tale-types, while others are motifs. Using the classifications of the Tale-Type Index, we can identify the following of Gerould's themes:

Type 505	The grateful dead
Type 506	The rescued princess (= Gerould's the ransomed woman)
Type 507A	The monster's bride (= the poison maiden)
Type 507B	The monster in the bridal chamber
Type 507C	The serpent maiden
Type 508	The bride won in a tournament (= the spendthrift knight)
Type 513	The extraordinary companions (= the skillful companions)
Type 551	The sons on a quest for a wonderful remedy for their father (= water of life)
Type 554	The grateful animals

Other important elements in Gerould's analysis are now regarded as motifs, identified as follows in Thompson's Motif Index:

B 13	Helpful animal is an enchanted person
B 350	Grateful animals
B 560	Animals advise man
D 1500	Magic object controls disease
D 1500.1.18	Magic healing water
D 1505	Magic object cures blindness
E 0	Resuscitation
E 80	Water of life

E 340	Return from dead to repay obligation
E 341	Grateful dead
E 341.1	Dead grateful for having corpse ransomed
F 582	Poison damsel
F 582.1	Serpent damsel
H 972	Tasks accomplished with help of grateful dead
H 1210.1	Quest assigned by father
H 1233.4	Supernatural creature as helper on quest
H 1233.6	Animals help hero on quest
H 1241	Series of quests; one can be accomplished when second is finished, etc.
H 1242	Youngest brother alone succeeds on quest
H 1320	Quest for marvelous object or animals
H 1321.2	Quest for healing water
K 1932	Impostors claim reward earned by hero
K 2211	Treacherous brother
L 13	Compassionate youngest son
Q 2	Kind and unkind
Q 42.1	Spendthrift knight
S 268	Child sacrificed to provide blood for cure of friend
T 172	Dangers to husband in bridal chamber
T 172.0.1	All bridegrooms of princess have perished during bridal night
T 172.1	Bridal chamber filled with coiled snakes
T 172.2	Bridal chamber invaded by magic dragon/serpent
T 172.2.1	Grateful dead man kills princess's monster husband
V 62.1	Funeral rites forbidden
W 154.12.3	Ungrateful brothers plot against rescuer

Yet even with the aid of these tools, tale analysis is not easy. Note that "grateful dead," "grateful animals," and "serpent maiden [damsel]" themes are both tale types and motifs. More generally, one must decide whether a theme is the essence of the tale or only a contributing unit. This ambiguity is partly because the types are defined mainly by either character or a combination of character and action, while motifs are an assortment of characters, actions, attributes, and objects.

Gerould's analysis led him to the following general conclusions regarding the Grateful Dead tales. The theme of the Grateful Dead first appeared early in the first century C.E. or before, probably in western Asia, and soon was combined with the Poison Maiden theme, which came from India by way of Persia. It then migrated to other parts of Asia and Europe, where the combined form, Grateful Dead + Poison Maiden, merged with the Lady and the Monster theme. It independently became entwined with the Ransomed Woman theme sometime before the fourteenth century. By the sixteenth century, the Thankful Beasts and Water of Life themes had become mixed in with the others. These dates—fourteenth to sixteenth centuries—are the earliest for which we have any evidence; the combinations could have occurred hundreds of years earlier. The table at the end of this introduction shows that there are some regional clusterings of themes, but in general, geography is not a strong determinant of story types.

Because (possibly) the earliest appearance of the theme was in the Apocryphal book of *Tobit,* Gerould relied on it to establish its terminus ad quem. (By this, he seemed to be discounting the relevance of the Simonides anecdote.) When Gerould published his study, it was believed that *Tobit* had been written originally in Hebrew at the time of Emperor Hadrian (117–138 C.E.). Since *Tobit* has the Poison Maiden theme, Gerould concluded that the merging of the two themes must have occurred before *Tobit* was written, that is, by the end of the first century C.E. Because of this important role that the Apocryphal book plays in Gerould's analysis, it is worth noting the results of more recent scholarship, as summarized by Carey A. Moore in his introduction to the book of *Tobit* in the Anchor Bible.[28] The best evaluation now is that the book was written in Aramaic in the "eastern Diaspora"—that is, in Asia Minor—not earlier than approximately 300 B.C.E. This allows us to push back the beginnings of the Grateful Dead stories by at least three centuries and maybe more. Of course, it did not escape Gerould's notice that the Tobit story was unique in several ways, most significantly in that the helpful companion who accompanied Tobit's son, Tobias, on his quest was not the ghost of the deceased whom Tobit took pains to bury but was the angel Raphael. This strengthened the conclusion that the Grateful Dead story originated before the book was written, since it makes more sense that *Tobit*'s Jewish author deliberately made the change to inject a specific theological import to the work rather than that everyone else who picked up the story independently changed the angel into the spirit of the dead person.

Pushing back the date of *Tobit* does not alter any of Gerould's arguments. This is partly because there are no other appearances of the theme for some thousand years—until the Middle Ages. This gap in the fossil record is a decided handicap in trying to apply a historic-geographic comparative method.

There has been one substantial study of the Grateful Dead theme since Gerould's monograph: Sven Liljeblad's 1927 study.[29] Liljeblad took issue with some of Gerould's basic assumptions (e.g., the notion that complex tales grew out of the admixture of original simple themes technically denoted *urforms*) and conclusions (e.g., the historical relationship between the Grateful Dead tale and Poison Maiden and the Lady and the Monster tales).

Other variants of the tale have been recovered as recently as the 1960s. Liljeblad cited versions from the Caucasus, Finland, Palestine, and Malaysia published after Gerould's study. More Irish versions are cited by Tom Peete Cross;[30] a version has turned up in Egypt;[31] and Gerould would doubtless be pleased to learn that the Grateful Dead tale has also made an appearance in the United States—in Kentucky.[32] The one ballad incorporating the theme—"The Factor's Garland"—has also been found in the United States—in Texas, North Carolina, Vermont, and Michigan.[33] Consideration of such relatively late versions would probably not alter Gerould's conclusions. The absence of any tales from the Grimms' collections may surprise the reader; in fact, two Grateful Dead tales were sent to the Grimm brothers in 1812–14, but they were not included in any of the editions of their published collections.[34] I might also mention a recent children's version of one of the Grateful Dead tales, *The Water of Life*.[35]

Gordon Gerould's monograph did not attract great notice when it was first published. I have found no reviews of it, either popular or scholarly, and it was not mentioned among his publications in his obituary in the *New York Times*.[36] Yet, together with *The Ballad of Tradition*, it still represents Gerould's most important contribution to scholarship. It has twice before gone out of print and been republished.[37]

Without belaboring the relation of the folktales to the rock group, I cannot help but notice that recent interest in the folktales has been partially spurred by a passion for the rock group. (The publications cited in notes 2 and 33 were by authors who admired the rock group and became intrigued with the problem of the antecedent folktale.) The Grateful Dead stories enumerated in Gerould's study span a wide range of folktales with many variegated themes and motifs.

This reprint of *The Grateful Dead: The History of a Folk Story* should bring both a particular family of folktale themes and folktale scholarship in general to the attention of a new audience of enthusiasts. I sense that the dead Professor Gerould would be appropriately grateful.

Notes

1. According to one account, the name was taken from a "big dictionary" (David Shenk and Steve Silberman, eds., *Skeleton Key: A Dictionary for Deadheads* [New York: Doubleday, 1994], 120) or from a "big Oxford dictionary" (John Rocco, ed., *Dead Reckonings: The Life and Times of the Grateful Dead* [New York: Schirmer, 1999], 26). The expression does not appear in the *Oxford English Dictionary* or in most other unabridged dictionaries, but according to Shenk and Silberman, it is in

Funk and Wagnalls New Practical Standard Dictionary of the English Language, vol. 1 (New York: Funk and Wagnall, 1955). An alternative account would have it that the band's leader, Jerry Garcia, took the name from an Egyptian prayer he had read. See Donald Clarke, ed., *The Penguin Encyclopedia of Popular Music* (New York: Viking, 1989), 486.

2. Bob Franzosa, ed., *Grateful Dead Folktales* (Orono, Maine: Zosa-farm Publications, 1989). This is a retelling of thirteen Grateful Dead folktales with an introduction and brief annotations.

3. As far as I can tell, Gerould first used the phrase "grateful dead" but as a translation from the German. Perhaps the credit for being first should be given to Karl Simrock, whose *Der gute Gerhard und die dankbaren Todten; ein beitrag zur deutschen mythologies und sagenkunde* (Bonn: A. Marcus, 1856) was the first scholarly study of the tale family. George Stephens's *Ghost-Thanks or The Grateful Unburied: A Mythic Tale in Its Oldest European Form, Sir Amdace* (Cheapinghaven: Michaelsen and Tillge, 1860) should also be mentioned as an early contribution to the literature—and evidence of a different English term prior to Gerould.

4. Princeton University press release, 1 July 1946, Box 185, Dean of Faculty Records: Faculty Files, Princeton University Archives, Seeley G. Mudd Manuscript Library, Princeton University Library, Princeton, N.J.

5. Letter dated 23 February 1918, ibid.

6. Eulogy written by Albert M. Friend, Maurice W. Kelley, and Carlos Baker, chairman, ibid.

7. Francis James Child, *The English and Scottish Popular Ballads,* 5 vols. (1882–88; reprint, New York: Cooper Square Publications, 1965).

8. See K. Wilgus's superb history, *Anglo-American Ballad Scholarship since 1898* (New Brunswick, N.J.: Rutgers University Press, 1959).

9. Gordon Gerould, "The Making of Ballads," *Modern Philology* (Chicago) 21 (August 1923): 18.

10. Ibid., 23.

11. Ibid., 26–27.

12. Gordon Gerould, "The Ballad of 'The Bitter Withy,'" *PMLA* 23 (1908): 141–67. In *The Ballad of Tradition,* Gerould also argued that "The Blind Beggar of Bednall Green," "The Seven Virgins," "The Shooting of His Dear or Molly Bawn," "Over Yonder's a Park or Corpus Christi," "The Bold Fisherman," and "Bruton Town or The Bramble Briar" were

appropriate inclusions to the Child corpus.

13. Louise Pound, "A Recent Theory of Ballad Making," *PMLA* 44 (1929): 625.

14. Gordon Gerould, "The 'Popular' Ballad," *Literary Review*, 5 March 1921, 6.

15. Gordon Gerould, "'Tenting on the Old Camp Ground' and Its Composer," *New England Magazine* (Boston), August 1899, 723–31.

16. Percy Hutchinson, "Review of *The Ballad of Tradition*," *New York Times*, 12 June 1932, sect. v:2.

17. Reed Smith, "Review of *The Ballad of Tradition*," *Journal of American Folklore* 46 (April–June 1933): 195.

18. Gordon Gerould, *The Ballad of Tradition* (New York: Oxford University Press, 1932; reprint, New York: Gordian, 1974), 11.

19. Gordon Gerould, "Forerunners, Congeners, and Derivatives of the Eustace Legend," *PMLA* 19 (1904): 335–448.

20. Ibid., 336.

21. In two instances, Gerould seems to have introduced inconsistencies in his enumerations. On page 45, there are twenty-five, not twenty-four, stories listed; and on page 153, the "Lion de Bourges" is omitted from the list of "eleven" variants.

22. We should not take Gerould to task for failing to provide English translations of texts that he cites from Latin, German, or French; not only was he comfortable in those tongues, but most of his readership at the time was as well.

23. Cicero, *De Senectute, de Amicitia, de Divinatione,* with an English translation by William Armistead Falconer (New York: G. P. Putnam's Sons, 1927), book I, sect. 57.

24. See page 29, herein.

25. Ibid., 173.

26. Stith Thompson, *The Types of the Folktale: A Classification and Bibliography—Antti Aarne's Verzeichnis der Märchentypen,* 2d rev. ed. (Helsinki: Academia Scientiarum Fennica, 1964).

27. Stith Thompson, *Motif-Index of Folk-Literature: A Classification of Narrative Elements in Folktales, Ballads, Myths, Fables, Mediaeval Romances, Exempla, Fabliaux, Jest-Books, and Local Legends,* rev. and enl. ed., 6 vols. (Bloomington: Indiana University Press, 1955–58).

28. Carey A. Moore, *Tobit: A New Translation with Introduction and Commentary* (New York: Doubleday, 1996). A précis is given by Moore

in *The Oxford Companion to the Bible*, ed. Bruce M. Metzger and Michael D. Coogan (New York: Oxford University Press, 1993), 745–46.

29. Sven Liljeblad, *Die Tobiasgeschichte und andere Märchen mit Toten Helfern* (*The Tobias story and other tales with Dead Helpers*) (Lund: A.-B. Ph. Lindstedts Univ.–Bokhandel, 1927).

30. Tom Peete Cross, *Motif-Index of Early Irish Literature*, Folklore Series No. 7 (Bloomington: Indiana University Press, 1952), 215.

31. Hasan M. El-Shamy, *Folk Traditions of the Arab World: A Guide to Motif Classification*, vol. 1 (Bloomington: Indiana University Press, 1995), 114.

32. "Old Shake-Your-Head," in *Tales from the Cloud Walking Country*, by Marie Campbell (Bloomington: Indiana University Press, 1958), 98–100 (Type 507B). More references are given in D. L. Ashliman, *A Guide to Folktales in the English Language: Based on the Aarne-Thompson Classification System* (Westport, Conn.: Greenwood, 1987), 106–7.

33. See G. Malcolm Laws, *American Balladry from British Broadsides* (Philadelphia: American Folklore Society, 1957), 292 [Q 37] for references.

34. See "Der dankbare Tote und die aus der Sklaverei erlöste Königstochter," in *Anmerkungen zu den Kinder- U. Hausmärchen der Brüder Grimm*, vol. 3, by Johannes Bolte and Georg Polívka (Leipzig: Dieterich'sche Verlagsbuchhandlung, 1918), no. 217. For English translations, see "The Dead Man and the Princess Freed from Slavery" and "Dead Man's Thanks," in *Grimms' Other Tales*, selected by Wilhelm Hansen and translated and edited by Ruth Michaelis-Jena and Arthur Ratcliff (South Brunswick, N.J.: A. S. Barnes, 1959), 123, 126. Wilhelm Grimm regarded the first of these two tales as too much like a story from a book.

35. *The Water of Life: A Tale of the Grateful Dead*, retold by Alan Trist (Eugene, Ore.: Hulogos'i Communications, 1989).

36. *New York Times*, 12 April 1953, 88.

37. Krause Reprints, 1967; Folcroft Reprint, 1973 (edition limited to 100 copies).

Grateful Dead Folktales: Gerould's Bibliography

Variant	A.T.505 Grateful Dead	Miscellaneous Combinations	A.T.507 Poison Maiden	A.T.508 Spendthrift Knight	A.T.506 Ransomed Woman	A.T.551 Water of Life	A.T.554 Thankful Beast	A.T.513 Skillful Companions	Two Friends	Division of Children
1 Tobit			X							
2 Armenian (modern folktale, publ. 1856)	X		X							
3 Jewish (modern from Palestine, publ. 1880)	X						X			
4 Annamite [Vietnam] (publ. 1886)	X		X							
5 Siberian (Turkey?, publ. 1866)										
6 Simonides (from Cicero; cf. Nun's Priest's Tale)	X									
7 Gypsy (heard near Adrianople [W. Turkey], publ. 1870)	X		X							
8 Greek (northern Euboea, publ. 1864)	X	a								
9 Maltese (publ. 1904)	X									
10 Russian I (publ. ca. 1906)	X		X			X				
11 Russian II (publ. 1862)	X		X							
12 Russian III (publ. 1880)	X		X							
13 Russian IV (publ. 1831)	X		X							
14 Russian V (publ. 1893)	X		X							
15 Russian VI (publ. 1883)	X				X					
16 Servian I (publ. 1870)	X									
17 Servian II (publ. 1871)	X		X							
18 Servian III (publ. 1871)	X		X							
19 Servian IV (publ. 1863)	X	b	X				X			
20 Servian V (publ. 1883)	X									
21 Servian VI (publ. 1883)	X				X	X				
22 Bohemian (publ. 1860)	X					X				

#	Title	1	2	3	4	5	6	7	8
24	Bulgarian (publ. 1876)		X		X				X
25	Lithuanian I (publ. 1875)	X			X				
26	Lithuanian II (publ. ca. 1872)	X							
27	Hungarian I (publ. 1850)	X			X	X			
28	Hungarian II (publ. 1857)	X	X			X			
29	Rumanian I (publ. 1857)					X			
30	Rumanian II (publ. 1858)					X			
31	Transylvanian [Romania] (publ. 1856)				a				X
32	Esthonian I (publ. ca. 1862)	X	X			X			
33	Esthonian II (publ. 1830)	X	X						
34	Finnish (publ. 1866)	X							
35	Catalan (publ. 1872)	X			X				
36	Spanish (publ. 1849–51)	X			X				
37	Lope de Vega (Spain, publ. 1623), taken from Oliver	X			X				
38	Calderon (Spain, publ. 1610?), taken Lope de Vega	X		X				X	X
39	Trancoso (Portugal, publ. 1575)	X			X			X	
40	Nicholas (French, publ. 1480)	X			X				
41	Richars (Picardy, France, or eastwards, written 13th c.)	X		X	X				
42	Lion de Bourges (French, 14th c. ms.)	X		X					
43	Oliver de Castille (French, publ. 1472)	X		X	X			X	X
44	Jean de Calais I (Brittany, publ. 1723)	X			X				X
45	Jean de Calais II (Gascony, publ. 1866)	X			X		X		X
46–48	Jean de Calais III, IV, V (Gascony, publ. ca. 1880)	X			X				X
49	Jean de Calais VI (Brittany; publ. 1882)	X			X				X

Continued on next page

Gerould's Bibliography (continued)

Variant	A.T.505 Grateful Dead	Miscellaneous Combinations	A.T.507 Poison Maiden	A.T.508 Spendthrift Knight	A.T.506 Ransomed Woman	A.T.551 Water of Life	A.T.554 Thankful Beast	A.T.513 Skillful Companions	Two Friends	Division of Children
50 Jean de Calais VII (Basque, publ. 1877)	X				X		X			X
51 Jean de Calais VIII (Brittany, publ. 1902)	X				X					X
52 Jean de Calais IX (Asturia, Spain, publ. 1886)	X				X					X
53 Jean de Calais X (Wallonia, ç publ. 1891)	X				X		X			
54 Walewein (= Gawain; Dutch, from France, publ. 1846)	X					X	X			
55 Lotharingian (Lorraine, publ. 1886)						X	X			
56 Gasconian (publ. 1861)	X				X					
57 Dianese (Italy, 14th c.)	X			X						
58 Stellante Costantina (Italy; not discussed further)	X									
59 Straparola I (Italian novelist's retelling, publ. 1550–53)	X				X					
60 Straparola II (Italian novelist's retelling, publ. 1550–53)						X				
61 Tuscan (Pistoia region of Italy, publ. 1880)	X				X	X	X	X		
62 Istrian (Italy, publ. 1880)	X				X	X				
63 Venetian (publ. 1875)	X					X				
64 Sicilian (publ. 1870)						X				
65 Brazilian (publ. 1885)	X					X				
66 Basque I (publ. 1877)	X						X			
67 Basque II (publ. 1877)	X				X		X			X
68 Gaelic (publ. 1890)	X				X					X

#	Version	1	2	3	4	5	6	7	8	9
69	Irish I (publ. 1893)	X	X	X			X		X	X
70	Irish II (publ. 1890)	X					X		X	X
71	Irish III (publ. 1866)	X					X		X	
72	Breton I (publ. 1874)	X		c						
73	Breton II (publ. 1881)	X			X		X			
74	Breton III (publ. 1881)	X				X	X			
75	Breton IV (publ. 1880)	X				X	X			
76	Breton V (publ. 1887)	X			X		X			X
77	Breton VI (publ. 1887)	X					X			
78	Breton VII (publ. 1887)	X					X		X	
79	Old Swedish (from 1265–70)	X		a	X		X	X		
80	Swedish (publ. 1819)	X					X			
81–82	Danish I, II (publ. 1854)	X	a						X	
83	Danish III (H. C. Andersen, publ. 1855, based on Norwegian II)	X								
84	Norwegian I (publ. 1868)	X			X		X			
85	Norwegian II (publ. 1855)	X	X		X		X		X	
86	Icelandic I (publ. 1864)	X			X			X		
87	Icelandic II (publ. 1902 from ms.)	X			X			X		
88	Rittertriuwe (14th c. poem)	X		X		X	X	X		
89	Treu Heinrich (publ. 1850)	X		X		X		X		
90	Simrock I (Rhineland, Germany, publ. 1851)	X		X	X	X	X	X		
91	Simrock II (Odenwald, Germany, publ. 1850s)	X			X	X	X			X
92	Simrock III (Swabia, Germany, publ. 1852)	X			X	X	X			X
93	Simrock IV (Germany, publ. 1853)	X			X	X	X			
94	Simrock V (Germany from Tyrol, publ. 1856)	X			X			X		
95	Simrock VI (Xanten, W. Germany, publ. 1856)	X			X		X			

Continued on next page

Gerould's Bibliography (continued)

Variant	A.T.505 Grateful Dead	Miscellaneous Combinations	A.T.507 Poison Maiden	A.T.508 Spendthrift Knight	A.T.506 Ransomed Woman	A.T.551 Water of Life	A.T.554 Thankful Beast	A.T.513 Skillful Companions	Two Friends	Division of Children
96 Simrock VII (Xanten, W. Germany, publ. 1856)	X				X	X				
97 Simrock VIII (Westphalia, Germany, publ. ca. 1856)	X				X		X			X
98 Simrock IX (Germany, publ. 1856)	X					X	X			
99 Simrock X (Rhineland, Germany, publ. 1856)	X		X			X	X			
100 Oldenburgian (publ. 1867)	X		X			X				
101 Harz I (Germany, publ. 1862)	X		X			X				
102 Harz II (Germany, publ. 1862)	X					X		X		
103 Sir Amadas (15th c. ms.)	X			X						X
104 Jack the Giant Killer (1711 earliest)	X		X			X				
105 Factor's Garland (18th c. English broadsides)	X				X					X
106 Old Wives' Tale (George Peele, 1590)	X		X			X				
107 Fatal Dowry (English play, Massinger & Field, 1652)	X									
108 Fair Penitent (English play, N. Rowe, 1720)	X									

a. Combined with Puss in Boots
b. Combined with swan maiden story
c. Combined with tale of Gregory the Great

PREFACE

THE combination of narrative themes is so frequent a phenomenon in folk and formal literature that one almost forgets to wonder at it. Yet in point of fact the reason for it and the means by which it is accomplished are mysteries past our present comprehension. If we could learn how and where popular tales unite, if we could formulate any general principle of union or severance, we should be well on the way to an understanding of the riddle which has hitherto baffled all students of narrative, namely, the diffusion of stories. We have theories enough; our immediate need is for more studies of individual themes, careful and, if it must be, elaborate discussions of many well-known cycles. Happily, these are accumulating and give promise of much useful knowledge at no distant day.

One principle has become clear. Since motives are so frequently found in combination, it is essential that the complex types be analyzed and arranged, with an eye kept single nevertheless to the master-theme under discussion. Collectors, both primary and subsidiary, have done such valiant service that the treasures at our command are amply sufficient for such studies, so extensive, indeed, that the task of going through them thoroughly has become too great for the unassisted student. It cannot be too strongly urged that a single theme in its various types and compounds must be made predominant in any useful comparative study. This is true when the sources and analogues of any literary work are treated; it is even truer when the bare motive is discussed.

The Grateful Dead furnishes an apt illustration of the necessity of such handling. It appears in a variety of different combinations, almost never alone. Indeed, it is so widespread a tale, and its combinations are so various, that there is the utmost difficulty in determining just what may properly be regarded the original kernel of it, the simple theme to which other motives were joined. Various opinions, as we shall see, have been held with reference to this matter, most of them justified perhaps by the materials in the hands of the scholars holding them, but none quite adequate in view of later evidence. The true way to solve the riddle appears to be this: we must ask the question,—what is the residuum when the tale is stripped of elements not common to a very great majority of the versions belonging to the cycle? What is left amounts to the following,—the story reduced to its lowest terms, I take it.

A man finds a corpse lying unburied, and out of pure philanthropy procures interment for it at great personal inconvenience. Later he is met by the ghost of the dead man, who in many cases promises him help on condition of receiving, in return, half of whatever he gets. The hero obtains a wife (or some other reward), and, when called upon, is ready to fulfil his bargain as to sharing his possessions.

Nowhere does a version appear in quite this form; but from what follows it will be seen that the simple story must have proceeded along some such lines. The compounds in which it occurs show much variety. It will be necessary to study these in detail, not merely one or two of them but as many as can be found. Despite the bewildering complexities that may arise, I hope that this method of approach may throw some new light on the wanderings of the tale.

Of my debt to various friends and to many books, though indicated in the body of the work, I wish to make general and grateful acknowledgment here. My thanks, furthermore, are due to the librarians of Harvard University for their courteous hospitality; to Professor G. L. Kittredge for his generous encouragement to proceed with this study, though he himself, as I found after most of my material was collected, had undertaken it several years before I began; and to Professor R. K. Root for his help in reading the proofs.

The Grateful Dead

To

Professor A. S. Napier

in Gratitude and Friendship

CHAPTER I.

A REVIEW.

To Karl Simrock is due the honour of discovering the importance of *The Grateful Dead* for the student of literature and legend. In his little book, *Der gute Gerhard und die dankbaren Todten*,[1] he called attention to the theme as a theme, and treated it with a breadth of knowledge and a clearness of insight remarkable in an attempt to unravel for the first time the mixed strands of so wide-spread a tale. Using the Middle High German exemplary romance, *Der gute Gerhard*, as his point of departure, he examined seventeen other stories, all but two of which have the motive well preserved.[2] Unhappily, the versions which he found came from a limited section of Europe, most of them from Germanic sources. Thus he was led to an interpretation of the tale on the basis of Germanic mythology. This, though ingenious enough and very erudite, need not detain us. It was done according to a fashion of the time, which has long since been discarded. Simrock took the essential traits of the theme to be the burial of the dead and the ransom from captivity.[3] "Wo nur noch eine von beiden das Thema zu bilden scheint," he said, "da hat die Ueberlieferung gelitten." Here again he was misled by the narrow

[1] 1856.
[2] *Guter Gerhard*, as will be seen later, does not follow the theme at all.
[3] P. 114.

A

range of his material, as later studies have shown. Nearly all the versions he cited have the motive of a ransomed princess, though the majority of the stories now known to be members of the cycle do not contain it. Three years after the publication of Simrock's monograph Benfey treated some features of the theme in a note appended to his discussion of *The Thankful Beasts* in the monumental *Pantschatantra*.[1] Though he named but a few variants, he found an Armenian tale which he compared with the European versions, coming to the conclusion not only that the motive proceeded from the Orient but also that the Armenian version had the original form of it. That is, he took the ransom and burial of the dead, the parting of a woman possessed by a serpent, and the saving of the hero on the bridal night as the essential features. This was a step in advance.

George Stephens in his edition of *Sir Amadas*[2] held much the same view. He added several important versions, and scored Simrock for admitting *Der gute Gerhard*, saying that he could not see that it had "any direct connection" with *The Grateful Dead*.[3] He was at least partly in the right, even though his statement was misleading. According to his opinion,[4] "the peculiar feature of the Princess (Maiden) being freed from *demonic* influence by *celestial* aid, is undoubtedly the original form of the tale."

In a series of notes beginning in the year 1858 Köhler[5] supplied a large number of variants, which have been invaluable for succeeding study of the theme. Nowhere,

[1] 1859, i. 219-221.

[2] *Ghost-Thanks or The Grateful Unburied, A Mythic Tale in its Oldest European Form, Sir Amadace*, 1860.

[3] P. 9.   [4] P. 7.

[5] *Germania*, iii. 199-210, xii. 55 ff. ; *Or. u. Occ.* ii. 322-329, iii. 93-103 ; *Arch. f. slav. Phil.* ii. 631-634, v. 40 ff. ; Gonzenbach, *Sicilianische Märchen*, 1870, ii. 248-250.

however, did he give an ordered account of the versions at his command or discuss the relation of the elements— a regrettable omission. The contributions of Liebrecht,[1] though less extensive, were of the same sort. In his article published in 1868 he said that he thought *The Grateful Dead* to be of European origin,[2] but he added nothing to our knowledge of the essential form of the story. The following decade saw the publication by Sepp of a rather brief account of the motive,[3] which was chiefly remarkable for its summary of classical and pre-classical references concerning the duty of burial. Like Stephens he assumed that the release of a maiden from the possession of demons was an essential part of the tale. In 1886 Cosquin brought the discussion one step further by showing [4] that the theme is sometimes found in combination with *The Golden Bird* and *The Water of Life.* He did not, however, attempt to define the original form of the story nor to trace its development.

By all odds the most adequate treatment that *The Grateful Dead* has yet received is found in Hippe's monograph, *Untersuchungen zu der mittelenglischen Romanze von Sir Amadas,* which appeared in 1888.[5] Not only did he gather together practically all the variants mentioned previous to that time and add some few new ones, but he studied the theme with such interpretative insight that anyone going over the same field would be tempted to offer an apology for what may seem superfluous labour. Such a follower, and all followers, must gratefully acknowledge their indebtedness to his labours.

[1] *Heidelberger Jahrbücher der Lit.* 1868, lxi. 449-452, 1872, lxv. 894 f. ; *Germania,* xxiv. 132 f.

[2] P. 449.

[3] *Altbayerischer Sagenschatz zur Bereicherung der indogermanischen Mythologie,* 1876, pp. 678-689.

[4] *Contes populaires de Lorraine,* i. 214, 215.

[5] *Archiv f. d. Stud. d. neueren Sprachen,* lxxxi. 141-183.

Yet one who follows imperfectly the counsels of perfection may discover certain defects in Hippe's work. He neglects altogether Cosquin's hint as to the combination of the theme with *The Water of Life* and allied tales, thus leaving out of account an important element, which is intimately connected with the chief motive in a large number of tales. Indeed, his effort to simplify, commendable and even necessary as it is, brings him to conclusions that in some respects, I believe, are not sound. Though he states the essential points of the primitive story in a form [1] which can hardly be bettered and which corresponds almost exactly to the one that I have been led to accept from independent consideration of the material,[2] he fails to see that he is dealing in almost every case, not with a simple theme with modified details but with compound themes. Thus he starts out with the " Sage vom dankbaren Toten und der Frau mit den Drachen im Leibe "[3] and explains all variations from this type either by the weakening of this feature and that or by the introduction of a single new motive, the story of *The Ransomed Woman*. He would thus make it appear[4] that we have a well-ordered progression from one combined type to various other combined and simplified types. Such a series is possible without doubt, but it can hardly be admitted till the interplay of all accessible themes, which have entered into combination with the chief theme, is investigated. Hippe passes these things

---

[1] P. 167. " Ein Jüngling zeigt sich menschenfreundlich gegen die Leiche eines Unbekannten (indem er dieselbe vor Schimf bewahrt, bestattet, etc.). Der Geist des Toten gesellt sich darauf zu ihm und erweist sich ihm dankbar, indem er ihm zu Reichtum und zum Besitze des von ihm zur Frau begehrten Mädchens verhilft, jedoch unter der Bedingung, dass er dereinst alles durch ihn Gewonnene mit ihm teile. Der Jüngling geht auf diesen Vertrag ein, und der Geist stellt sich nach einer gewissen Zeit wieder ein, um das Versprochene entgegenzunehmen, verlangt aber nicht die Hälfte des gewonnene Gutes, sondern die der Frau. (Schluss variabel.)"

[2] See p. x. above.　　　　[3] P. 180.　　　　[4] See his scheme on p. 181.

over silently and so gives the subject a specious air of simplicity to which it has no right.

I should be the last to deny the necessity of treating narrative themes each for itself, and I have nothing but admiration for the general conduct of Hippe's investigation ; but I wish to show that his methods, and therefore his results, are at fault in so far as he does not recognize the nature of the combinations into which *The Grateful Dead* enters. Traces of other stories, unless their presence is obviously artificial, must be carefully considered, since in dealing with cycles of such fluid stuff as folk-tales it is certainly wise to give each element due consideration. Certain minor errors in Hippe's article will be mentioned in due course, though my constant obligations to it must be emphasized here.

Since the appearance of Hippe's study no one has treated *The Grateful Dead* with such scope as to modify his conclusions. Perhaps the most interesting work in the field has been that of Dr. Dutz[1] on the relation of George Peele's *Old Wives' Tale* to our theme. He follows Hippe's scheme, but gives some interesting new variants. Of less importance, but useful within its limits, is the section devoted to the saga by Dr. Heinrich Wilhelmi in his *Studien über die Chanson de Lion de Bourges.*[2] Though he added no new versions, the author studied in detail the relationship of some of the mediaeval forms to one another, basing his results for the most part on careful textual comparison. His gravest fault was the thoroughly artificial way in which he mapped out the field as a whole, a method which could lead only to erroneous conclusions, since he classified according to a couple of superficial traits. An English study by Mr. F. H. Groome on *Tobit and Jack the*

---

[1] *Der Dank des Todten in der englischen Literatur, Jahresbericht der Staats-Oberrealschule in Troppau,* 1894.

[2] Marburg diss. 1894, pp. 43-63.

Giant-Killer[1] unhappily was written without regard to the previous literature of the subject, and simply rehearses a number of well-known variants.

In this brief review I have touched only on such studies of *The Grateful Dead* as have materially enlarged the knowledge of the subject or have attempted a discussion of the theme in a broad way. In the following chapter reference will be made to other works, in which particular versions have been printed or summarized.

[1] *Folk-Lore*, ix. 226-244 (1898).

CHAPTER II.

BIBLIOGRAPHY.

THE following list of variants of *The Grateful Dead* includes only such tales as have the fundamental traits. as sketched above, either expressed or clearly implied, Thus *Der gute Gerhard*, for example, is not mentioned because it has only the motive of *The Ransomed Woman*, while one of the folk-tales from Hungary is admitted because it follows in general outline one of the combined types to be discussed later, even though the burial of the dead is obscured. I cite by the short titles which will be used to indicate the stories in the subsequent discussion. The arrangement is roughly geographical.

TOBIT.

In the apocryphal book of *Tobit*. According to Neubauer, *The Book of Tobit, a Chaldee Text from a unique MS. in the Bodleian Library*, 1878, p. xv, *Tobit* was originally written in Hebrew, although the Hebrew text preserved was taken from Chaldee. Neubauer (p. xvii) quotes Graetz, *Geschichte der Juden*, (2nd ed.) iv. 466, as saying that the book was written in the time of Hadrian, and he concludes that it cannot be earlier because it was unknown to Josephus. The correspondence with *Sir Amadas*, and thus with *The Grateful Dead* generally, seems to have been first noted by Simrock, p. 131 f., again by Köhler, *Germania*, iii. 203, by Stephens, p. 7, by Hippe, p. 142, etc.

ARMENIAN.

A. von Haxthausen, *Transkaukasia*, 1856, i. 333 f. A modern folk-tale. Reprinted entire by Benfey, *Pantschatantra*, i. 219, note, and by Köhler, *Germania*, iii. 202 f. A somewhat inadequate summary is given by Hippe, p. 143 ; a better one is found in *Arch. f. slav. Phil.* v. 43, by Köhler, who mentioned the tale again in *Or. und Occ.* ii. 328, and iii. 96. Summarized also by Sepp, p. 681, Groome, *Folk-Lore*, ix. 228 f., and mentioned by Wilhelmi, p. 45.

JEWISH.

Reischer, *Schaare Jeruschalajim*, 1880, pp. 86-99. Summarized by Gaster, *Germania*, xxvi. 200-202, and from him by Hippe, pp. 143, 144. A modern folk-tale from Palestine.

ANNAMITE.

Landes, *Contes et légendes annamites*, 1886, pp. 162, 163, " La reconnaissance de l'étudiant mort." A modern folk-tale.

SIBERIAN.

Radloff, *Proben der Volkslitteratur der türkischen Stämme Süd-Siberiens*, 1866, i. 329-331. See Köhler, *Arch. f. slav. Phil.* v. 43, note.

SIMONIDES.

Cicero, *De Divinatione*, i. 27, referred to again in ii. 65 and 66. Retold by Valerius Maximus, *Facta et Dicta*, i. 7 ; after him by Robert Holkot, *Super Libros Sapientie*, Lectio 103 ; and again by Chaucer in the *Nun's Priest's Tale, Cant. Tales*, B, 4257-4294. For the relationship of Chaucer's anecdote to those in Latin see Skeat, note in his edition, Lounsbury, *Studies in Chaucer*, 1892, ii. 274, and Petersen, *On the Sources of the Nonne Prestes Tale*, 1898, pp. 106-117. Connected with *The Grateful Dead* by Freudenberg in a review of Simrock in *Jahrbücher des Vereins von Alterthumsfreunden im Rheinlande*, xxv. 172. See also Köhler, *Germania* iii. 209, Liebrecht in *Heidelberger Jahrbücher der Lit.* lxi. 449, 450, and Sepp. p. 680. Not treated by Hippe.

GYPSY.

A. G. Paspati, *Études sur les Tchinghianés ou Bohémiens de l'Empire Ottoman*, 1870, pp. 601-605, Translated from Paspati by F. H. Groome, *Gypsy Folk-Tales*, 1899, pp. 1-3. Summarized by Köhler, *Arch. f. slav. Phil.* v. 43 and carelessly by Hippe, p. 143. This tale was heard near Adrianople. Cited by Foerster, *Richars li Biaus*, p. xxviii, and by Wilhelmi, p. 45.

GREEK.

J. G. von Hahn, *Griechische und albanesische Märchen*, 1864, no. 53, pp. 288-295, "Belohnte Treue." Summarized in part by Hippe, p. 149. See also Liebrecht, *Heid. Jahrbücher*, lxi. 451, and by Groome, *Folk-Lore*, ix. 243. This tale was found in northern Euboea.

MALTESE.

Hans Stumme, *Maltesische Märchen, Gedichte und Rätsel*, 1904, no. 12, pp. 39-45.

RUSSIAN I.

Afansjew, *Russische Volksmärchen*, Heft 6, p. 323 f. Analyzed by Schiefner, *Or. und Occ.* ii. 174, 175, and after him by Hippe, p. 144, with some omissions. See Köhler, *Or. und Occ.* iii. 93-103, and Sepp, p. 684.

RUSSIAN II.

Chudjakow, *Grossrussische Märchen*, Heft 3, pp. 165-168. Translation by Schiefner, *Or. und Occ.* iii. 93-96 in article by Köhler. In English by Groome, *Folk-Lore*, ix. 229 ff. Summarized by Köhler, *Arch. f. slav. Phil.* v. 43, and (with an important omission) by Hippe, pp. 144, 145. See Köhler's notes in Gonzenbach, *Sicilianische Märchen*, ii. 250.

RUSSIAN III.

Reproduced from an illustrated folk-book in the *Publications of the Society of Friends of Old Literature in St. Petersburg*, 1880, no. 49. Summarized by V. Jagić, *Arch. f. slav. Phil.* v. 480, and by Hippe, p. 145. Jagić remarks that the tale must have been widely known in Russia in the eighteenth century, though clearly of foreign origin.

RUSSIAN IV.

Dietrich, *Russische Volksmärchen in den Urschrift gesammelt*, 1831, no. 16, pp. 199-207. English translation, *Russian Popular Tales. Translated from the German Version of Anton Dietrich*,

1857, pp. 179-186. "Sila Zarewitsch und Iwaschka mit dem weissen Hemde." Like other tales in the collection this was taken from a popular print bought at Moscow. Mentioned by Benfey, *Pantschatantra*, i. 220, and by Köhler, *Or. u. Occ.* ii. 328.

RUSSIAN V.[1]

P. V. Šejn, *Materialien zur Kenntniss der russischen Bevölkerung von Nordwest-Russland*, 1893, ii. 66-68, no. 33. Cited by Polívka in *Arch. f. slav. Phil.* xix. 251.

RUSSIAN VI.

P. V. Šejn, *work cited*, ii. 401-407, no 227. Cited by Polívka, *Arch. f. slav. Phil.* xix. 262.

SERVIAN I.

Vuk Stefanović Karadžić, 2nd ed. of his Servian folk-tales, 1870. Translated by Madam Mijatovies (Mijatovich), *Serbian Folk-Lore*, 1874, p. 96. Summarized from Servian by Köhler, *Arch. f. slav. Phil.* ii. 631, 632, and from him by Hippe, p. 145.

SERVIAN II.

Summarized from Gj. K. Stefanović's collection, 1871, no. 15, by Jagić in *Arch. f. slav. Phil.* v. 40 f. with the title "Vlatko und der dankbare Todte." Thence by Hippe, p. 145.

SERVIAN III.

Jagić in *Arch. f. slav. Phil.* v. 41 f, from Stojanović's collection, no. 31. Hippe's summary, p. 146, is exceedingly brief and faulty.

SERVIAN IV.

Jagić, *Arch. f. slav. Phil.* v. 42, from *Matica*, B. 105 (A.D. 1863, St. Novaković). Summary of this by Hippe, p. 146. Jagić calls the tale "Ein Goldfisch."

SERVIAN V.

Krauss, *Sagen und Märchen der Südslaven*, 1883, i. 385-388, "Der Vilaberg." Summarized by Dutz, p. 11.

---

[1] I have to thank the kindness of Professor Leo Wiener for my knowledge of the content of *Russian V.* and *VI.*, which he was good enough to translate for me from the dialect of White Russia.

SERVIAN VI.

Krauss, *work cited*, i. 114-119. "Fuhrmann Tueguts Himmelswagen." From the manuscript collection of Valjavec. Summarized by Dutz, p. 18, note 2.

BOHEMIAN.[1]

Waldau, *Böhmisches Märchenbuch*, 1860, pp. 213-241. Mentioned by Köhler, *Or. und Occ.* ii. 329, and by Hippe, p. 146. Summarized by the former, *Oc. und Occ.* iii. 97 f.

POLISH.

K. W. Wójcicki, *Klechdy, Starożytne podania i powieści ludowe*, 2nd ed., Warsaw, 1851. Translated into German by F. H. Lewestam, *Polnische Volkssagen und Märchen*, 1839, pp. 130 ff; into English by A. H. Wratislaw, *Sixty Folk-Tales from exclusively Slavonic Sources*, 1889, pp. 121 ff.; and into French by Louis Leger, *Recueil de contes populaires slaves*, 1882, pp. 119 ff. Summarized by Köhler, *Germania*, iii. 200 f., and by Hippe, pp. 146 f. See also Sepp, p. 684, Dutz, p. 11, Groome, *Gypsy Folk-Tales*, p. 3, note, and Arivau, *Folk-Lore de Proaza*, 1886, p. 205.

BULGARIAN.

Lydia Schischmánoff, *Légendes religieuses bulgares*, 1896, no. 77, pp. 202-209,[2] "Le berger, son fils, et l'archange."

LITHUANIAN I.

L. Geitler, *Litauische Studien*, 1875, pp. 21-23. Analyzed by Köhler, *Arch. f. slav. Phil.* ii. 633, and after him briefly by Hippe,[3] p. 147, as his "Lithuanian II."

LITHUANIAN II.

Köhler, *Arch. f. slav. Phil.* ii. 633 f. From Prussian Lithuania. Summarized by Hippe, p. 147, as his "Lithuanian III."

---

[1] What the two Bohemian variants contain, which are mentioned by Benfey, *Pantschatantra*, i. 221, note, by Stephens, p. 10, by Köhler, *Germania*, iii. 199-209, and *Or. und Occ.* ii. 328, note, and by Hippe, p. 146, I have been unable to ascertain.

[2] On pp. 194-201 is found a curious "Écho de l'histoire de Tobie."

[3] Hippe's first Lithuanian tale is a variant of *The Water of Life* and will be treated in another connection.

HUNGARIAN I.

G. Stier, *Ungarische Sagen und Märchen*, 1850, pp. 110-122. Mentioned by Köhler, *Germania*, iii. 202, and by Hippe, p. 147.

HUNGARIAN II.

G. Stier, *Ungarische Volksmärchen*, 1857, pp. 153-167. Summarized by Köhler, *Germania*, iii. 199 f., and too briefly by Hippe, p. 148.

RUMANIAN I.

Arthur Schott, *Neue walachische Märchen*, in Hackländer and Hoefer's *Hausblätter*, 1857, iv. 470-473. Mentioned by Stephens, p. 10, Hippe, p. 147, and Benfey, *Pantschatantra*, ii. 532.

RUMANIAN II.

F. Obert. *Romänische Märchen und Sagen aus Siebenbürgen*, in *Das Ausland*, 1858, p. 117. Mentioned by Köhler, *Germania*, iii. 202, and by Hippe, p. 147.

TRANSYLVANIAN.

Haltrich, *Deutsche Volksmärchen aus dem Sachsenlande in Siebenbürgen*, 1856, pp. 42-45. Analyzed by Köhler, *Or. und Occ.* ii. 326, and incompletely by Hippe, p. 148. Mentioned by Stephens, p. 10, and Sepp, p. 684.

ESTHONIAN I.

Schiefner, *Or. und Occ.* ii. 175 f., whence the analysis by Hippe, p. 148.

ESTHONIAN II.

Reisen in mehrere russische Gouvernements in den Jahren 1801, 1807 und 1815, 1830, v. 186-192, from *Ein Ausflug nach Esthland im Junius 1807*. Reprinted by Kletke, *Märchensaal*, 1845, ii. 60-62. Summarized by Dutz, p. 18, note 3.

FINNISH.

Liebrecht, *Germania*, xxiv. 131, 132. Communicated by Schiefner from *Suomen, Kansan Satuja*, Helsingfors, 1866. Summarized by Hippe, pp. 148 f.

CATALAN.

F. Maspons y Labrós, *Lo Rondollayre: Quentos populars catalans*, Segona Série, 1872, no. 5, pp. 34-37. Analyzed by

Liebrecht, *Heid. Jahrbücher der Lit.* lxv. 894 (1872), and after him by Hippe, p. 151. Mentioned by d'Ancona, *Romania,* iii. 192, and by Foerster, *Richars li Biaus,* p. xxviii.

SPANISH.

Duran, *Romancero general,* 1849-51, ii. 299-302, nos. 1291, 1292. Summarized by Köhler, *Or. und Occ.* ii. 323 f. and after him by Cosquin, *Contes populaires,* i. 215, and by Hippe, p. 151.[1] Mentioned by Sepp, p. 686.

LOPE DE VEGA.

Comedy in two parts, *Don Juan de Castro.* According to J. R. Chorley, *Catálogo de comedias y autos de Frey Félix de Vega Carpio,* p. 5, this play is to be found in Part xix. of the *Comedias* published in 1623 (later issues 1624, 1625, and 1627). A. Schaeffer, *Geschichte des spanischen Nationaldramas,* 1890, i. 141, says that the second part, called *Las aventuras de don Juan de Alarcos,* is in Part xxv. of Lope's comedies. The entire play is edited by Hartzenbusch, *Comedias Escogidas de Lope de Vega,* iv. 373 ff. and 395 ff. in the *Biblioteca de autores españoles,* lii. Schaeffer, pp. 141, 142, gives a careful summary of the play, and Köhler, *Or. und Occ.* iii. 100 f., gives another. The latter is followed by Hippe, p. 151. Mentioned by Duran, *Romancero general,* ii. 299, by Sepp, p. 686, and by Wilhelmi, pp. 45 ff. and 60.

CALDERON.

El Mejor Amigo el Muerto, by Luis de Belmonte, Francisco de Rojas, and Pedro Calderon de la Barca, in *Biblioteca de autores españoles,* xiv. 471-488, and in *Comedias escogidas de los mejores ingenios de España,* 1657, ix. 53-84. Analyzed by Köhler, *Or. und Occ.* iii. 100 f., and briefly after him by Hippe, p. 151. Mentioned by Sepp, p. 686, and by Wilhelmi, pp. 60 f. Schaeffer, *work cited,* ii. 283 f., says that a play of this name was written by Belmonte alone in 1610, which was revised about 1627 with the aid of Rojas and Calderon.

---

[1] Hippe speaks of "zwei spanische Romanzen." Had he consulted the Spanish text or read Köhler's note more attentively, he would have seen that a single story runs through nos. 1291 and 1292 of the *Romancero.*

TRANCOSO.[1]

Contos e historias de proveito e exemplo, by Gonçalo Fernandez Trancoso, Parte 2, Cont. ii., first published in 1575 and frequently re-issued during the sixteenth and seventeenth centuries. In the edition published at Lisbon in 1693, our tale is found on pp. 45r.-6or.; and in that published at the same place in 1710, on pp. 110-177. Menéndez y Pelayo, *Orígenes de la Novela (Nueva Biblioteca de autores españoles* vii.), 1907, ii. lxxxvii ff., gives a bibliography, the table of contents, and a description of the work on the basis of seventeenth century editions; on p. xcv. he connects the tale above-mentioned with *The Grateful Dead.* See T. Braga, *Contos tradicionaes do povo portuguez,* 1883, ii. 63-128, who prints nineteen of the tales in abbreviated form, but not ours.

NICHOLAS.

Johannes Junior (Gobius), *Scala Celi,* 1480, under *Elemosina.* Gobius was born in the south of France and lived about the middle of the fourteenth century.[2] Summary by Simrock, pp. 106-109. Mentioned by Hippe, p. 169.

RICHARS.

Richars li Biaus, ed. W. Foerster, 1874. A romance written in Picardy or eastwards in the thirteenth century (Foerster, p. xxi). Analyzed by Köhler, *Revue critique,* 1868, pp. 412 ff., and Hippe, p. 155. Compared in detail with *Lion de Bourges* by Wilhelmi, pp. 46 ff.

LION DE BOURGES.

An Old French romance known to exist in two manuscripts, the earlier dating from the fourteenth century,[3] the later from

---

[1] My attention was called to this variant by the kindness of Professor F. De Haan, and I was supplied with a first summary from the 1693 edition by the friendly aid of Professor G. T. Northup.

[2] See Crane, *Exempla of Jacques de Vitry,* 1890, p. lxxxvi.

[3] P. Paris, *Manuscrits françois,* 1840, iii. 1, and Foerster, *Richars li Biaus,* 1874, p. xxvii, date it from the fifteenth century; Suchier, *Oeuvres poétiques de Philippe de Beaumanoir,* 1884, p. lxxxiv, and Wilhelmi, p. 15, from the fourteenth century.

about the end of the fifteenth.[1] It has never been edited, but the portion which concerns us was analyzed in detail by Wilhelmi, pp. 18-38. This summary I have made the basis of my discussion. The romance was mentioned by P. Paris, Foerster, and Suchier (as cited in note below), Gautier, *Les épopées françaises*, 1st ed. 1865, i. 471-473, Ebert, *Jahrbuch f. rom. und engl. Lit.* iv. 53, 54, and Benfey, *Pantschatantra*, i. 220. A prose translation into German is found in manuscripts of the fifteenth century, which does not differ materially from the original.[2] This was printed in 1514, and summarized by F. H. von der Hagen, *Gesammtabenteuer*, 1850, i. xcvii-xcix, Simrock, pp. 104-106, and Hippe, p. 154. See E. Müller, *Überlieferung des Herpin von Burges*, 1905, who analyzes the work and treats its relations to *Lion*.

OLIVER.

Olivier de Castille et Artus d'Algarbe, a French prose romance composed before 1472, according to Foulché-Delbosc (*Revue hispanique*, ix. 592). The first and second editions were printed at Geneva, the first in 1482, the second before 1492.[3] There exist at least three manuscripts of the work from the fifteenth century : MS. Bibl. nat. fran. 12574 (which attributes the romance to a David Aubert, according to Gröber, *Grundriss der rom. Phil.* ii. 1, 1145); MS. Brussels 3861 ; and Univ. of Ghent, MS. 470. The designs of the last have been reproduced, together with a summary of the text, by Heins and Bergmans, *Olivier de Castille*, 1896. An English translation was printed by Wynkyn de Worde in 1518. A translation from the second French edition into Castilian was made by Philippe Camus, which was printed thirteen times between 1499 and 1845.[4] The edition of 1499 has lately been reproduced in facsimile by A. M. Huntington, *La historia de los nobles caualleros Oliueros de castilla y artus dalgarbe*, 1902. A German translation from the French was made by Wilhelm Ziely in 1521, and this was translated into English by Leighton and Barrett, *The History of Oliver and Arthur*, 1903. From the

---

[1] P. Paris, *place cited*, and Foerster, *place cited*, say the sixteenth century, but Wilhelmi, *place cited*, the fifteenth.

[2] See Wilhelmi, p. 43.   [3] Foulché-Delbosc, pp. 589, 590.

[4] *Work cited*, pp. 587, 588.

German prose Hans Sachs took the material for his comedy on the theme (publ. 1556). A summary of Ziely's work is given by Frölicher, *Thüring von Ringoltingen's "Melusine," Wilhelm Ziely's " Olivier und Artus" und " Valentin und Orsus,"* 1889, pp. 65 f., which is used by Wilhelmi, pp. 55, 56, in his comparison of the romance with *Richars* and *Lion de Bourges.* An Italian translation, presumably from the French, was printed three or four times from 1552 to 1622.[1] A summary of the story is given in *Mélanges tirés d'une grande bibliothèque*, by E. V. 1780, pp. 78 ff., with an incorrect note about the romance, reproduced by Hippe, pp. 155 f., with an analysis from the same source of the part of the tale belonging to our cycle. Robert Laneham in his list of ballads and romances, made in 1575, mentions *Olyuer of the Castl.* See Furnivall, *Captain Cox, his Ballads and Books*, Ballad Soc. 1871, vii. xxxvii and 30.

JEAN DE CALAIS.

I. Mme. Angélique de Gomez, *Histoire de Jean de Calais*, 1723. Sketched in the *Bibliothèque universelle des romans*, Dec. 1776, pp. 134 ff. Köhler, *Germania*, iii. 204 ff., gives a summary of the work, which Mme de Gomez stated was "tiré d'un livre qui a pour titre : *Histoire fabuleuse de la Maison des Rois de Portugal.*" A later anonymous redaction of this *Jean de Calais* exists in prints of 1770, 1776, and 1787, and it continued to be issued in the nineteenth century. Summarized by Hippe, pp. 156 f., and by Sepp, pp. 685 f. Mentioned by Köhler in Gonzenbach, *Sicil. Märchen*, ii. 250.

II. Bladé, *Contes populaires de la Gascogne*, 1886, ii. 67-90. This and the following folk-versions of *Jean* deserve careful consideration because of the interesting character of their variations.

III. J. B. Andrews, *Folk-Lore Record*, iii. 48 ff., from Mentone. See Liebrecht, *Engl. Stud.* v. 158, and Hippe, p. 157.

IV. and V. J. B. Andrews, *Contes ligures, traditions de la Rivière*, 1892, pp. 111-116, no. 26, and pp. 187-192, no. 41. These two versions differ slightly from one another, but more from the preceding.

[1] *Place cited.*

VI. P. Sébillot, *Contes populaires de la Haute-Bretagne,* 3me. série, 1882, pp. 164-171.

VII. Wentworth Webster, *Basque Legends,* 1877, pp. 151-154. See Luzel, *Légendes chrétiennes,* p. 90, note.

VIII. A. Le Braz, *La légende de la mort chez les Bretons armoricains,* nouv. éd., 1902, ii. 211-231.

IX. L. Giner Arivau, *Folk-Lore de Proaza* (Asturia), in *Biblioteca de las tradiciones populares españolas,* viii. 194-201 (1886).

X. Gittée and Lemoine, *Contes populaires du pays Wallon,* 1891, pp. 57-61.

WALEWEIN.

Roman van Walewein, ed. Jonckbloet, 1846. Analyzed by G. Paris, *Hist. litt. de la France,* xxx. 82-84, and by W. P. Ker, *The Roman van Walewein (Gawain)* in *Folk-Lore,* v. 121-127 (1894). My analysis is a combination made from these two summaries.

LOTHARINGIAN.

Cosquin, *Contes populaires de Lorraine,* 1886, i. 208-212 (no. xix). Noted by Hippe, p. 157.

GASCONIAN.

Cénac Moncaut, *Contes populaires de la Gascogne,* 1861, pp. 5-14, "Rira bien qui rira le dernier." Summarized by Köhler, *Or. und Occ.* ii. 329. Mentioned by Hippe, p. 157, and by Groome, *Folk-Lore,* ix. 239.

DIANESE.

Novella di Messer Dianese e di Messer Gigliotto, ed. d'Ancona and Sforza, 1868. Analyzed by Liebrecht, *Heid. Jahrbücher der Lit.* lxi. 450 (1868), by d'Ancona, *Romania,* iii. 191, (reprinted in his *Studj di critica e storia,* 1880, p. 353), and by Hippe, p. 152. D'Ancona's summary is from Papanti, nov. xxi. The variant is of the fourteenth century, according to the writer of the introduction of the edition of 1868, p. 5. See also Foerster, *Richars li Biaus,* p. xxiv, and Wilhelmi, pp. 44 and 57.

STELLANTE COSTANTINA.

D'Ancona, *Romania,* iii. 192, mentions the popular poem *Istoria bellissima di Stellante Costantina figliuola del gran turco, la quale fu rubata da certi cristiani che teneva in corte suo padre e fu venduta*

B

a un mercante di Vicenza presso Salerno, con molti intervalli e successi, composta da Giovanni Orazio Brunetto. I have not been able to find this poem and do not know how closely it accords with *Dianese.*

STRAPAROLA I.

Notti piacevoli, notte xi, favola 2. Analyzed by Grimm, *Kinder- und Hausmärchen*, 1856, iii. 289; and rather too briefly by Simrock, pp. 98-100, and Hippe, p. 153. See Benfey, *Pant.* i. 221, Köhler in Gonzenbach, *Sicil. Märchen*, ii. 249, and Groome, *Tobit and Jack*, *Folk-Lore*, ix. 226 f., and *Gypsy Folk-Tales*, p. 3, note.

STRAPAROLA II.

Notti piacevoli, notte v, favola 1. See Benfey, *Pant.* ii. 532.

TUSCAN.

G. Nerucci, *Sessanta novelle popolari*, 1880, pp. 430-437, no. lii. A folk-tale from the neighbourhood of Pistoia. See Webster, *Basque Legends*, pp. 182-187, Crane, *Italian Popular Tales*, p. 350, and Cosquin, *Contes populaires*, i. 215.

ISTRIAN.

Ive, *Novelline popolari rovignesi*, 1877, p. 19. See d'Ancona, *Studj di critica*, 1880, p. 354, and the summary by Crane, *Italian Popular Tales*, 1885, no. xxxv. pp. 131-136, from whom, as Ive's collection has been inaccessible to me, I derive my knowledge of the story. Crane gives the title of Ive as *Fiabe*, etc., d'Ancona as above.

VENETIAN.

G. Bernoni, *Tradizioni populari veneziane*, 1875, pp. 89-96. Referred to by Crane, *Italian Popular Tales*, p. 350.

SICILIAN.

Laura Gonzenbach, *Sicilianische Märchen*, 1870, ii. 96-103. Summarized briefly by Hippe, pp. 153 f., and by Groome, *Folk-Lore*, ix. 239 f.

BRAZILIAN.

Roméro and Braga, *Contos populares do Brazil*, 1885, no. x. pp. 215. See Cosquin, *Contes populaires*, i. 215.

BASQUE I.

Wentworth Webster, *Basque Legends*, 1877, pp. 182-187. See Cosquin, *Contes populaires*, i. 215, and Luzel, *Légendes chrétiennes,* p. 90, note.

BASQUE II.

Webster, *work cited*, pp. 146-150. See Crane, *Italian Popular Tales*, p. 351.

GAELIC.

Campbell, *Popular Tales of the West Highlands*, new ed. 1890, ii. 121-140, no. 32, "The Barra Widow's Son." Summarized by Köhler, *Or. und Occ.* ii. 322 f., by Sepp, p. 685, by Hippe, p. 150, and by Groome, *Folk-Lore*, ix. 235. See Köhler in Gonzenbach, *Sicil. Märchen*, ii. 249, and Groome, *Gypsy Folk-Tales*, p. 3, note.

IRISH I.

W. Larminie, *West Irish Folk-Tales and Romances*, 1893, pp. 155-167, "Beauty of the World." Mentioned by Kittredge, *Harvard Notes and Studies*, viii. 250, note.

IRISH II.

Douglas Hyde, *Beside the Fire. A Collection of Irish Gaelic Folk-Stories*, 1890, pp. 18-47, "The King of Ireland's Son."[1] Mentioned by Kittredge, *place cited.*

IRISH III.

P. Kennedy, *Legendary Fictions of the Irish Celts*, 1866, pp. 32-38, "Jack the Master and Jack the Servant."

BRETON I.

Souvestre, *Le foyer breton, contes et récits populaires*, nouv. ed. 1874, ii. 1-21. Analyzed by Simrock, pp. 94-98, by Sepp, p. 685, and in part by Hippe, p. 149. See Luzel, *Légendes chrétiennes*, i. 90, note.

BRETON II.

F. M. Luzel, *Légendes chrétiennes de la Basse-Bretagne*, 1881, i. 68-90, "Le fils de Saint Pierre." Cited by von Weilen, *Zts. f.*

[1] My attention was first called to this story by the kindness of Professor A. C. L. Brown.

vergl. Litteraturgeschichte, N.F. i. 105. Analyzed in part by Hippe, pp. 149 f.

BRETON III.

Luzel, *work cited,* ii. 40-58. Mentioned by von Weilen, *place cited,* and analyzed by Hippe, p. 150. The title, slightly misquoted by Hippe, is " Cantique spirituel sur la charité que montra Saint-Corentin envers un jeune homme qui fut chassé de chez son père et sa mère, sans motif ni raison."

BRETON IV.

P. Sébillot, *Contes populaires de la Haute-Bretagne,* 1880, pp. 1-8. Noted by Luzel, *work cited,* p. 90, note, and by Cosquin, *Contes populaires,* i. 215.

BRETON V.

F. M. Luzel, *Contes populaires de Basse-Bretagne,* 1887, ii. 176-194, " La princesse Marcassa."

BRETON VI.

F. M. Luzel, *work cited,* ii. 209-230, "La princesse de Hongrie."

BRETON VII.

F. M. Luzel, *work cited,* i. 403-424, " Iouenn Kerménou, l'homme de parole."

OLD SWEDISH.

Stephens, pp. 73 f., reprinted with translation from his *Ett Forn-Svenskt Legendarium,* 1858, ii. 731 f. This variant from 1265-1270 is analyzed by Hippe, pp. 158 f.

SWEDISH.

P. O. Bäckström, *Svenska Folkböcker,* 1845-48, ii. 144-156, from H—d (Hammarsköld) and I—s (Imnelius), *Svenska Folksagor,* 1819, i. 157-189. Bäckström also cites several editions of the folk-book, which he says is of native origin. Mentioned by Stephens, p. 8. Summarized by Liebrecht, *Germania,* xxiv. 130 f., and by Hippe, p. 158.

DANISH I.

S. Grundtvig, *Gamle Danske Minder i Folkemunde,* 1854, pp. 77-80, " Det fattige Lig." Mentioned by Stephens, p. 8, by

Hippe, p. 160, and by Wilhelmi, p. 45. Summarized by Köhler, *Or. und Occ.* iii. 99.

DANISH II.

Grundtvig, *work cited,* pp. 105-108, "De tre Mark." Summarized by Köhler, *Or. und Occ.* iii. 100. Cited by Hippe, p. 160, and Wilhelmi, p. 45.

DANISH III.

Andersen, "Reisekammeraten," in *Samlede Skrifter,* xx. 54 ff. (1855). Found in most English editions of Andersen's tales as "The Travelling Companion." Based on *Norwegian II.* Analyzed by Sepp, p. 678. Cited by Köhler, *Or. und Occ.* ii. 327, by Hippe, p. 159, and by Groome, *Gypsy Folk-Tales,* p. 3, note.

NORWEGIAN I.

Asbjörnsen, *Iuletraeet,* 1866, no. 8, and *Norske Folke-Eventyr,* 1871, no. 99, pp. 198-201. Summarized by Liebrecht, *Heid. Jahrbücher der Lit.* lxi. 451 (1868), and by Hippe, p. 159. See Liebrecht, *Germania,* xxiv. 131.

NORWEGIAN II.

Asbjörnsen, *Illustreret Kalender,* 1855, pp. 32-39, *Iuletraeet,* no. 9, and *Norske Folke-Eventyr,* no. 100, pp. 201-214. Translated by Dasent, *Tales from the Fjeld,* 1874, pp. 71-88. Cited by Stephens, p. 8, Liebrecht, *Germania,* xxiv. 131, and Groome, *Gypsy Folk-Tales,* p. 3, note. Somewhat inadequate summaries by Liebrecht, *Heid. Jahrbücher der Lit.* lxi. 452, Hippe, p. 159, and Groome, *Folk-Lore,* ix. 230.

ICELANDIC I.

Árnason, *Íslenzkar þjóðsögur og Æfintýri,* 1864, ii. 473-479. English translation in Powell and Magnússon, *Legends Collected by Jón. Arnason,* 1866, pp. 527-540. German translation in Poestion, *Isländische Märchen,* 1884, p. 274. Cited by Liebrecht. *Heid. Jahrbücher,* lxi. 451, and *Germania,* xxiv. 131, and by Wilhelmi, p. 45. Summary by Köhler, *Or. und Occ.* iii. 101 f., and by Hippe, p. 159.

ICELANDIC II.

A. Ritterhaus, *Die neuisländischen Volksmärchen,* 1902, no. 57, pp. 232-235. From MS. 537, Landesbibliothek, Reykjavík.

RITTERTRIUWE.

F. H. von der Hagen, *Gesammtabenteuer*, 1850, i. 105-128, no. 6. A poem of 866 lines from the fourteenth century. Summaries in Benfey, *Pant.* i. 221, in Simrock, pp. 100-103, and, with a rather bad error, in Hippe, p. 164. See Foerster, *Richars li Biaus*, p. xxiv. Compared with *Richars, Oliver*, and *Lion de Bourges* by Wilhelmi, pp. 56 f.

TREU HEINRICH.

Der Junker und der treue Heinrich, ed. K. Kinzel, 1880. Previously edited and analyzed by von der Hagen, *Gesammtabenteuer*, iii. 197-255, no. 64. Summary by Simrock, pp. 103 f. Cited by Hippe, p. 165.

SIMROCK I.

J. W. Wolf, *Deutsche Hausmärchen*, 1858, pp. 243-250, contributed by W. von Plönnies. Summary by Simrock, pp. 46-51, by Köhler, *Or. und Occ.* iii. 98, and by Sepp, p. 683. Cited by Hippe, p. 165.

SIMROCK II.

W. von Plönnies in *Zts. f. deutsche Myth.* ii. 373-377. From the Odenwald. Summary by Simrock, pp. 51-54. See Hippe, p. 165. This is the story analyzed by Sepp, p. 688 f., though he also refers to Wolf's and Zingerle's tales.

SIMROCK III.

E. Meier, *Deutsche Volksmärchen aus Schwaben*, 1852, no. 42. pp. 143-153. Summarized by Simrock, pp. 54-58, Köhler, *Or, und Occ.* iii. 99, and Sepp, pp. 686 f. See Hippe, p. 165.

SIMROCK IV.

H. Pröhle, *Kinder- und Volksmärchen*, 1853, pp. 239-246. Summary by Simrock, pp. 58-62. See Hippe, p. 165.

SIMROCK V.

Simrock, pp. 62-65, contributed by Zingerle, who afterwards printed it in the *Zts. f. deutsche Myth.* ii. 367 ff., in *Sagen, Märchen und Gebräuche aus Tirol*, 1859, pp. 444 f., and in *Kinder- und Hausmärchen aus Tirol*, 2nd ed., 1870, pp. 261-267. Analyzed without mention of source by Sepp, pp. 687 f. See Hippe, p. 165.

SIMROCK VI.

Simrock, pp. 65-68, from Xanten. See Hippe, p. 165.

SIMROCK VII.

Simrock, pp. 68-75, from Xanten. See Hippe, p. 165.

SIMROCK VIII.

F. Woeste, *Zts. f. deutsche Myth.* iii. 46-50, from Grafschaft Mark. Given by Simrock, pp. 75-80. Analyzed by Sepp, p. 685, who inadvertently speaks of it as "nach irischer Sage." See Hippe, p. 165.

SIMROCK IX.

Simrock, pp. 80-89, contributed by Zingerle, who afterwards printed it in *Sagen, Märchen und Gebräuche aus Tirol,* 1859, pp. 446-450, and in *Kinder- und Hausmärchen aus Tirol,* 2nd ed., 1870, pp. 254-260. See Stephens, p. 9, Hippe, pp. 165 f., and Wilhelmi, p. 45.

SIMROCK X.

Simrock, pp. 89-94, from the foot of the Tomberg. Summarized by Köhler, *Or. und Occ.* ii. 326. See Hippe, p. 166, and Wilhelmi, p. 45.

OLDENBURGIAN.

L. Strackerjan, *Aberglaube und Sagen aus dem Herzogtum Oldenburg,* 1867, ii. 308 ff. Cited by Hippe, p. 166, and by Foerster, *Richars li Biaus,* p. xxviii.

HARZ I.

A. Ey, *Harzmärchenbuch,* 1862, pp. 64-74. Summary by Köhler, *Or. und Occ.* iii. 96. Cited by Hippe, p. 166.

HARZ II.

A. Ey, *work cited,* pp. 113-118. Summary by Köhler, *Or. und Occ.* iii. 97. Cited by Hippe, p. 166.

SIR AMADAS.

Ed. Weber, *Metrical Romances,* 1810, iii. 241-275, Robson, *Three Early English Metrical Romances,* 1842, pp. 27-56, Stephens, *Ghost-Thanks,* 1860. Stephens seems to have been the first to note the connection of *Sir Amadas* with *The Grateful Dead.* The romance, as it is preserved in two manuscripts of the fifteenth century, must accordingly have been composed as early as the second half of the preceding century. It contains 778 verses in the tail-rhyme stanza. Summarized by Köhler, *Or. und Occ.* ii. 325, by Foerster, *Richars li Biaus*, pp. xxiv-xxvi, by Groome, *Folk-Lore*, ix. 236, and by Hippe (with great care), pp. 160-164. Compared with *Oliver* by Wilhelmi, pp. 58 f.

JACK THE GIANT KILLER.

Found without essential difference in several chapbooks, the earliest owned by the British Museum being entitled: *The Second Part of | Jack and the Giants. | Giving a full Account of his victorious Conquests over | the North Country Giants; destroying the inchanted | Castle kept by Galligantus; dispersed the fiery Grif- | fins; put the Conjuror to Flight; and released not | only many Knights and Ladies, but likewise a Duke's | Daughter, to whom he was honourably married.* Newcastle-on-Tyne, 1711.[1] Other editions with the story are: *The History of Jack and the Giants*, Aldermary Churchyard, London; same title, Bow Church Yard, London; same title, Cowgate, Edinburgh; *The Pleasant and delightful History of Jack and the Giants*, Nottingham, Printed for the Running Stationers, and *The Wonderful History of Jack the Giant-Killer*, Manchester, Printed by A. Swindells; all without date. The Newcastle edition was reprinted by Halliwell-Phillipps in *Popular Rhymes and Nursery Tales*, 1849, in which our tale appears at pp. 67-77. Apparently the British Museum copy dated 1711 is that owned by Halliwell-Phillipps. From his edition it has been reprinted by Groome, *Folk-Lore*, ix. 237 f., and summarized by Köhler, *Or. und Occ.* ii. 327 f., and Sepp, p. 685. See also Stephens, p. 8. Hippe, p. 164, and Wilhelmi, p. 45.

FACTORS' GARLAND.[2]

The Factor's Garland or *The Turkey Factor*, a tale in English verse, which may be regarded as a popular ballad, though by no

---

[1] An edition with an almost identical title " Printed and sold by Larkin How, in Petticoat Lane," of which a copy is in the Harvard College Library, does not contain our story.

[2] My attention was called to this variant by the kindness of Professor Kittredge.

means as a primitive one. It has often been reprinted as a chapbook or broadside. The library of Harvard University possesses copies of no less than eight different editions (see W. C. Lane, *Catalogue of English and American Chap-Books and Broadside Ballads in Harvard College Library*, 1905, nos. 809-815, 2420). An examination of these shows that they differ from each other in no essential point, though they vary considerably in statements of time. The British Museum *Catalogue of Printed Books* lists seven editions, all different from those at Harvard, with one possible exception. The popularity of the story, at one time at least, is thus strikingly illustrated. Another variant, reported from oral tradition, has been found in North Carolina. See the paper read by J. B. .Henneman before the Modern Language Association of America on Dec. 29, 1906.

OLD WIVES' TALE.

George Peele, *The Old Wives' Tale* (1590), published in 1595, Ed. by Dyce, 1828 and 1861, by Bullen, 1888, and by Gummere in Gayley's *Representative English Comedies*, 1903, pp. 349-382. See H. Dutz for an elaborate discussion of the connection of the play with our theme.

FATAL DOWRY.

Philip Massinger (and Nathaniel Field), *The Fatal Dowry*. First printed in 1632. Ed. A. Symons, Mermaid Series, 1889, ii. 87-182.

FAIR PENITENT.

Nicholas Rowe, *The Fair Penitent, The Dramatick Works of Nicholas Rowe Esq.*, 1720, vol. i.

CHAPTER III.

TALES WITH THE SIMPLE THEME AND MIS-
CELLANEOUS COMBINATIONS.

OF the tales enumerated in the previous chapter, over one hundred in number, all but seventeen fall into well-defined categories as having *The Grateful Dead* combined with one or more of three given themes : *The Possessed Woman*, *The Ransomed Woman*, and *The Water of Life*. Of these seventeen variants, moreover, only four can be regarded as having the simple motive of *The Grateful Dead ;* and they are in part doubtful members of the family.

The first of them is *Simonides*, thus related by Cicero : " Unum de Simonide : qui cum ignotum quendam proiectum mortuum vidisisset eumque humavisset haberetque in animo navem conscendere, moneri visus est ne id faceret ab eo, quem sepultura adfecerat ; si navigavisset, eum naufragio esse periturum ; itaque Simonidem redisse, perisse ceteros, qui tum navigavissent." The source of Cicero's story we do not know, but in all probability it was Greek. Whether it really belongs to our cycle, being so simple in form and nearly two centuries earlier in date than any other version yet unearthed, is a matter for very great doubt. It may have arisen quite independently of other similar tales in various parts of the world, and have no essential connection with our tale ; but it deserves special consideration, not only from its antiquity, but also from its subsequent history in lineal descent through Valerius

Maximus, and possibly Robert Holkot[1] to Chaucer. We are at least justified in looking for some influence of so well-known an anecdote upon better-authenticated members of the cycle.

The three other variants with the simple theme are all folk-tales of recent gathering. The first of them is *Jewish,*[2] which runs as follows : The son of a rich merchant of Jerusalem sets off after his father's death to see the world. At Stamboul he finds hanging in chains the body of a Jew, which the Sultan has commanded to be left there until his co-religionists shall have repaid the sum that the man is suspected of having stolen from his royal master. The hero pays this sum, and has the corpse buried. Later during a storm at sea he is saved by a stone on which he is brought to land, whence he is carried by an eagle back to Jerusalem. There a white-clad man appears to him, explaining that he is the ghost of the dead, and that he has already appeared as stone and eagle. The spirit further promises the hero a reward for his good deed in the present and in the future life.

The second variant is the *Annamite* tale. Two poor students were friends. One died and was buried by the other, whose fidelity was such that he remained three years by the tomb. He dreamed that his friend came to him and said that he should gain the title of *trang nguyen*. So he built a chapel by the tomb, where the dead friend often appeared to him. When the king heard of his loyalty, he was praised and rewarded with a title. After his

---

[1] Miss Petersen's conclusion, *Sources of the Nonne Prestes Tale*, p. 109, note, is not altogether convincing, since the vogue of Valerius Maximus was so great that other authors than Holkot are likely to have quoted Cicero's stories from him. The book may yet be found in which the one follows the other " right in the nexte chapitre."

[2] Given by Hippe, pp. 143 f. Wherever Hippe's summaries are adequate and careful, I shall refer the reader to his monograph for comparison.

death the two friends appeared to their son and daughter, bidding them marry.[1]

The third story is *Servian VI.* An uncle of Adam, who honoured God and the "Vile,"[2] was so good a man that God came to him in human form one day. After a battle between the good and evil in the world, the latter would not bury the slain. The Vile told Tuegut that this would not do, so he hitched up his wagon and carried the slain to their graves. Then God came to earth, told him to put all he possessed in his wagon, and carried him on a cloud to heaven, where he was made the constellation now called Driver Tuegut's Heavenly Wagon.

Of these three tales the *Annamite* does not fulfil the usual condition that the dead man shall be a stranger to the one who does the good action. Together with *Simonides*, all of them vary widely in the reward given the hero. In *Simonides* he is warned against embarkation, and thus saved from shipwreck ; in the *Jewish* he is actually rescued from a storm-tossed vessel by the ghost, which masquerades as a rock and an eagle, and afterward promises him further rewards here and hereafter ; in the *Annamite* he is provided with earthly glory; and in *Servian VI.* he becomes a part of the galaxy of heaven. Only the underlying idea is the same,—that the burial of the dead is a pious act and a sacred duty, which will meet a fitting reward.[3] This belief is so widespread and ancient that it is not difficult to surmise how stories inculcating the duty might have grown up independently in many lands. At the same time, the very diversity of reward in these simple tales allies them to one or another of the compound types, which, though

---

[1] This story has nothing in common with the mediaeval tale of the compact between two friends that the first to die shall appear to the other. See the writer's *North-English Homily Collection*, 1902, pp. 27-31.

[2] Apparently beneficent spirits, whose nature is half fairy and half angel. See *Servian V.* below.

[3] See chapter viii. and Sepp, pp. 678-680 for illustrations of the belief.

multiform and widespread, are yet unmistakably the off-spring of a single parent form, or better, of a chance union between two motives.[1] Thus *Simonides* and *Jewish* recall the combination of *The Grateful Dead* with *The Ransomed Woman*, since they have the hero rescued from drowning by the ghost, and they suggest one point of union between the two themes. It therefore seems best to include them in our list, not only for the sake of completeness, but because they point to the reason which sometime and somewhere gave rise to a more developed form of the motive,—to the *märchen* as we shall study it. A consideration of these basal principles can be undertaken, however, only after the story theme in its various ramifications and modifications has been thoroughly discussed.

The probability that *The Grateful Dead* once existed in a simple, uncompounded form, which became the parent on one side of the more important combined types, is strengthened by the minor compounds in which it is found. How can the correspondences of detail seen in a considerable number of different compounds, as far as they run parallel, be otherwise explained? Surely it is more reasonable to believe in the existence of such a parent form than to suppose that an originally complicated form was hacked and hewn asunder to produce new compounds. This will become clearer, I hope, as we proceed.

In *Greek*, a boy was sold to a pasha, who betrothed him to his daughter. Because of the mother's objections, however, he was sent away as a shepherd, while the girl was promised to another pasha's son. The hero fed his flock under the shelter of the castle, and was summoned by the maiden, who gave him her betrothal ring in a

---

[1] One can conceive of separate generation of a very simple story under similar conditions, but not, I think, that a series of events showing combination of themes or detailed correspondence would so arise.

beaker, though pretending not to know him. The next
day she asked her parents to let the two suitors go into the
world with a thousand piasters apiece, and see which came
back with the most money. So they were sent forth. The
pasha's son remained in a city enjoying his money, while
the shepherd went on till he met an old man, to whom he
told his story. The man gave him a thousand piasters
more, and told him to buy an ape in a town hard by. He
succeeded in doing this, and brought the ape back to the old
man, who cut it in pieces, much to the youth's disgust, and
made eye-salve of the brain. With this he sent the hero
away after exacting a promise of half of what was obtained.
The youth won a thousand piasters by curing the blind,
and later a great sum, besides thirty ships, by healing a
very rich man. With this wealth he returned to the old
man, and with him to the city where the pasha's son had
sojourned. The latter agreed to let the shepherd's seal be
burned on his arm in return for the payment of his debts ;
but, while the hero and the old man sailed home, he rode
fast by land with the story that his rival was dead. The
shepherd arrived at home just in time for his rival's
wedding, and at the end of it showed the bride her ring.
She recognised her lover, called her parents, and, after
the hero had told his story and proved it by the seal on his
rival's arm, married him. That night the old man knocked
on the door of their chamber, and demanded that the bride
be divided. According to his promise, the hero prepared
to cut her in twain, when the intruder said that he wished
only to test his fidelity, explaining that he was God,
Who had taken him under His protection because his
father had sold him in order to keep the lamp burning
in honour of his saint.

In this variant the elements of *The Grateful Dead* have
been merged with a story about how a young man of low
birth won a princess by overcoming another suitor in spite
of the treachery of the latter. As I have met with but one

example of this, from Lesbos,[1] I will summarise it briefly. A princess becomes enamoured of the son of her father's gardener, and refuses to marry the son of the first minister. So the two suitors are sent out to a far country with the understanding that the one who returns first shall have the princess. On the way the gardener's son helps an old beggar-woman, whom his rival has spurned, and is told by her how to cure a sick king (by boiling him and sprinkling him with a certain powder). For this service the youth obtains a ring of bronze, which has the virtue of giving whatever its possessor desires. By means of this he gets a wonderful ship, and sails to the city where the minister's son, through extravagance, has fallen into poverty. He provides him with a wretched ship, in which to return home, on condition that he may mark him with his ring. The minister's son reaches home in his crazy vessel, and is about to marry the princess, when the hero appears on his beautiful ship of gold, exposes his rival, and weds the lady. The remainder of the story, which tells how the magical ring was lost and afterward recovered, does not concern us. It will be seen that *Greek* has preserved only the later part of *The Grateful Dead* at all clearly, though that combination with a tale of the type of the Lesbian narrative has actually taken place is evident from the part which the helper plays. He not only obtains a promise of division, but calls for its fulfilment. His first appearance is, however, quite unmotivated, while the old woman of the Lesbian story serves the purpose, according to a common formula, of showing the hero's kindness in contrast to his rival's hard heart. The point common to the two tales, which led to their combination, is without doubt this helping friend.

In *Servian V.* a youth on a journey pays his all to rescue a debtor from hanging. By his new-found friend

---

[1] Carnoy and Nicolaides, *Traditions populaires de l'Asie Mineure*, 1889, pp. 57-74.

the youth is led to the wondrous Vilaberg, where he is left with the admonition that he must not speak. He disobeys, and is made dumb and blind by an enchantress; but he is cured by the man whom he rescued, who plays on a pipe and gives him a healing draught. So he dwells for some years in the mountain with one of the ladies as his wife, but afterward goes home, though every summer he returns to his friends in the Vilaberg.

Here we have our theme combined with a form of *The Swan-Maiden*,[1] which occurs in only one other case, as far as I am able to discover. The reason for the combination is not far to seek. The latter part of the tale represents the reward of the rescuer by the rescued. That the benefit does not take the form of actual burial need not disturb us. The man was at least far gone towards death, and he was a debtor—a trait found in about two-thirds of the variants known to me. Moreover, the supernatural character of the comrade is indicated by the adventure into which he leads the youth. The tale has been partly rationalised, that is all.

Esthonian I.[2] shows a different combination, which is unique as far as I know. In a gorge not far from the village of Arukäla (near Wesenberg) a howling was heard every night for years. Finally a bold man went by night to the place and found the skeleton of a murdered king, which told him that it had howled thus for a hundred years because it had not been buried with holy rites. The next day the man took the bones to a priest, and, while burying them, discovered an enormous treasure.

As Schiefner said,[3] when he first printed the story, it recalls the Grimms' *Der singende Knochen*,[4] which in turn is

---

[1] See Baring-Gould's *Curious Myths*, 2nd ed. 1869, pp. 561 ff. for a popular account. The philosophical basis of the tale is discussed by Liebrecht, *Zur Volkskunde*, 1879, pp. 54 ff. (from *Germania*, xiii. 161 ff.), and by Hartland, *Science of Fairy Tales*, 1891, pp. 255-332, 337-347.

[2] See Hippe, p. 148.   [3] *Or. und Occ.* ii. 176.

[4] *Kinder- und Hausmärchen*, no. 28. See notes (ed. 1856), iii. 55, 56; also Köhler, *Kleinere Schriften*, i. 49, 54.

a compound of *The Water of Life*, with the idea of murder discovered by means of a dead man's bones. The Esthonian tale has, however, only the latter circumstance, combined with a simple form of *The Grateful Dead*. The hero's reward is immediate—he finds gold in the earth while digging the grave; and the ghost does not appear. The variant is thus of no great significance.

The group of tales that must next be considered furnishes rather more important evidence as to the development of the theme. It is a compound of *The Grateful Dead* with the motive which we may call *The Spendthrift Knight*. As far as I know, the type is purely mediaeval. The group includes *Richars*, *Lion de Bourges*, *Dianese*, *Old Swedish*, *Rittertriuwe*, and *Sir Amadas*.

The plot of *Richars*, as far as it concerns us, runs thus : Richars, in the pursuit of knightly exercises, wastes all his father's property as lord of Mangorie. When he hears that the King of Montorgueil has promised the hand of his daughter to the victor in a tourney, he is sad at the thought of his inability to engage. Through the generosity of a provost, however, he is enabled to set out with a horse, three attendants, and a supply of gold. At the city of Osteriche he spends part of his money in giving a great feast. In the roof of the house where he stays he is astonished to see a corpse lying on two beams, and he learns that it is the body of a knight, who died owing the householder three thousand pounds. Richars gives everything he has, even to his armour, to secure the release and burial of the dead man. He then proceeds to the tourney on a poor horse that his host gives him, and quite alone, since his attendants have deserted him. On the way he is joined by a White Knight, who offers him help in the tourney and places at his disposal his noble steed. Richars wins the tourney

c

and obtains the hand of the Princess Rose. He now offers the White Knight his choice of the lady or the property. The stranger, however, refuses any division, explains that he is the ghost of the indebted knight, and disappears.[1]

Lion de Bourges runs thus: Lion, son of Duke Harpin de Bourges, was found by a knight in a lion's den and reared as his son. When he grew up, he wasted his foster-father's property in chivalry. Finally, he heard that King Henry of Sicily had promised the hand of his daughter to the knight who should win a tourney that he had established. So Lion started for the court, and on the way ransomed the body of a knight, which he found hanging in the smoke, on account of unpaid debts. At Montluisant the hero won the favour of the Princess Florentine, and, before the tourney, obtained from a White Knight the charger which he still lacked, on condition of sharing his winnings, the princess excepted. With the help of this knight Lion was victorious and obtained the princess. He was then asked by his helper to give up either the lady or the whole kingdom, and did not hesitate to do the latter. At this, the stranger explained that he was the ghost of the ransomed knight and disappeared, though he afterwards returned to assist the hero at need.

---

[1] See Hippe, p. 155. This analysis includes only the second of two well-defined parts. The first section is related to the English *Sir Degarre* (ed. from Auchinleck MS. for the Abbotsford Club, 1849; from Percy Folio, Hales and Furnivall, *Percy Folio MS.*, 1868, iii. 16-48; early prints by Wynkyn de Worde, Copland, and John King; see G. Ellis, *Specimens of Early English Metrical Romances*, 1811, iii. 458 ff., J. Ashton, *Romances of Chivalry*, 1887, pp. 103 ff., Paul's *Grundriss*, ii. i. 643). This connection was pointed out by Foerster, p. xxiii. The same material was used also in a Dutch chapbook, *Jan wt den vergiere*, of which a copy printed at Amsterdam is preserved at Göttingen. See the article "Niederländische Volksbücher," by Karl Meyer, in *Sammlung bibliothekswissenschaftlicher Arbeiten*, ed. Dziatzko, viii. 17-22, 1895. I am indebted for this last reference to the kindness of Dr. G. L. Hamilton.

According to *Dianese*,[1] the knight of that name has wasted his substance. When he hears that the King of Chornualglia (Cornwall) has promised his daughter and half of his kingdom to the knight who wins the tourney that he has called, Dianese gets his friends to fit him out and sets forth. On the way he passes through a town where the traffic is diverted from the main street because of a corpse which has long been lying on a bier before a church. He learns that it is the body of a knight, who cannot be buried till his creditors have been paid. At the cost of everything he possesses, save his horse, the hero satisfies the creditors and has the knight buried. When he has gone on two miles, he is joined by a merchant, who promises him money, horses, and weapons if he will give in return half of what he wins in the tourney. Dianese agrees, is fitted out anew, and succeeds in overcoming all comers in the contest. Thus he obtains the hand of the princess and half the kingdom. With his bride, the merchant, and his followers he starts for home; but, when they are only a day's journey from their destination, he is required by the merchant to fulfil his promise—to choose between his bride as one half, his possessions as the other. Dianese takes the lady and rides on. Soon, however, he is joined by the merchant, who praises his faithfulness, gives up the treasures, explains that he is the ghost of the debtor knight, and disappears.

In *Old Swedish*[2] the daughter and heiress of the King of France promises to marry whatever knight is victor in a tourney which she announces. Pippin, the Duke of Lorraine, hears of this and sets out for France. At the end of his first day's journey he finds lodging at the house of a widow, who is lamenting because her husband, once in good circumstances, has died so poor that she cannot bury him properly. Pippin takes pity on her, and pays for the man's funeral. On his further journey he falls in with a man on a noble steed, who gives him the horse on condition of receiving half of whatever he shall win. Unthinkingly Pippin agrees and wins the tourney with the help of the horse. After he has married the princess, he is asked by the helper to fulfil his promise. He offers at first half, then the whole of his kingdom, in order to keep his bride, and is finally told by the man that he is the ghost of the dead, while the horse was an angel of God.

Rittertriuwe is of the same romantic character. . When Graf Willekin von Montabour had spent his substance in chivalrous exercises, he learned that a beautiful and rich maiden had promised her hand to the knight, who should win a tourney, which she had established. Thereupon he set forth and came to the place announced for the combats. There he found lodging in the house of a man, who would only receive him if he would promise to pay the debts of a dead man, whose body lay unburied in the dung of a horse-stall.[1] Willekin was moved by this story and paid seventy marks, almost all his money, to ransom the corpse and give it suitable burial. He then had to borrow from his host in order to indulge in his customary generosity. On the morning of the jousting he obtained from a stranger knight a fine horse on condition of dividing everything that he won. He succeeded in the tourney above all the other contestants, and so wedded the maiden. On the second night after the marriage the stranger entered his room and demanded a share in his marital rights. After he had offered instead to give all his possessions, the hero started from the room in tears, when the stranger called him back and explained that he was the ghost of the dead, then disappeared.

---

[1] This trait recalls the first of Chaucer's two stories in the *Nun's Priest's Tale*, *Cant. Tales*, B. 4174-4252, where the comrade is found buried with dung on a cart.

A brief summary of *Sir Amadas*,[1] the last of the six variants, must now be given. Amadas finds himself financially embarrassed, and sets forth for seven years of errantry with only forty pounds in hand. This he pays to release and bury the body of a merchant who has died in debt. When thus reduced to absolute penury, Amadas meets a White Knight, who tells him that he will aid him on condition of receiving half the gains. The hero finds a rich wreck on the seacoast, and so with new apparel goes to the court, where he wins wealth in a tourney and the princess's heart at a feast. After he marries her and has a son born to him, the White Knight reappears and demands that the accepted conditions be complied with. Hesitatingly Amadas prepares to divide first his wife and afterwards his son, but he is stayed by the stranger, who explains that he is the ghost of the dead merchant. So Amadas is at last released from misfortune and lives in happiness.

In all six of these stories we have a knight, who sets out to win a tourney in which the victor's prize is to be the hand of a princess. In all of them save *Old Swedish* he is represented as being impoverished by previous extravagance, in *Richars, Lion de Bourges,* and *Ritter-triuwe* it being expressly stated that he had wasted his fortune by over-indulgence in his passion for jousting. On his way to the place appointed for the contest the hero pays for the burial[2] of a man whose corpse is held for debt.[3] He goes on and is approached either before (*Richars, Lion de Bourges, Dianese, Old Swedish,* and *Sir*

---

[1] For a fuller analysis see Hippe, pp. 160-164.

[2] In *Richars, Lion de Bourges, Dianese,* and *Sir Amadas* he pays his all, even to his equipment for war, the most logical and, on the whole, probably the earlier form of the story.

[3] In all except *Old Swedish* and *Sir Amadas* the man was a knight; in these he was a merchant, the husband of the woman at whose house the hero lodges.

Amadas) or after (*Rittertriuwe*) he reaches the lists by a man, who provides him with a horse, by the aid of which he wins the tourney and the princess. In *Dianese* the hero is a merchant, in *Old Swedish* his estate is not mentioned, but in the other four variants he appears, as a knight (a white knight in *Richars, Lion de Bourges,* and *Sir Amadas*). In *Dianese* the hero is also provided with armour; in *Richars* and *Lion de Bourges* he is assisted in his jousting by the White Knight; and in *Sir Amadas* he finds a wreck on the coast from which he obtains all things needful. In *Richars* we find the somewhat inept conclusion that the hero asks his friendly helper whether he will take the princess or the property[1] as his share. The latter responds that he wishes only his horse, explains who he is, and vanishes. In all the other variants, however, the condition is made that the hero divide whatever he shall gain.[2]

With reference to *Richars* and *Lion de Bourges,* Wilhelmi's careful discussion[3] has made it clear that, though they agree in many points as against all the other related versions, not only in respect to *The Grateful Dead,* but to the further course of a complicated narrative, neither one could have been taken from the other. The difference in the matter of the division between *Richars* and all the other variants he neglects, though it strengthens his position. Back of *Richars* and *Lion de Bourges,* earlier than the thirteenth century, there must have existed a literary work which was their common source. This hypothetical French romance may be considered as the foundation of the whole group which we are discussing.

Since *Old Swedish* agrees with most of the other variants with regard to the division, and furthermore

---

[1] " V le femme u l'auoir ares," v. 5316.

[2] Though in *Lion de Bourges* he excepts the lady specifically.

[3] See *Über Lion de Bourges,* particularly pp. 46-54.

with *Rittertriuwe*, in stating that the hero offered all his property in order to keep his wife, there seems to be no doubt that it belongs to this particular group, despite the fact that it says nothing about the hero's poverty. The connection is not improbable on the score of chronology, if we suppose that the source of *Richars* and *Lion de Bourges*, or some similar tale, found its way into the North by translation in the first half of the thirteenth century, a time when translations into Icelandic at anyrate were made in great numbers. Indeed, the names Pippin, Lorraine, etc., immediately suggest a French source; and the story is not really a legend at all, though it appears in a legendary, but a narrative quite in the style of the *romans d'aventure*.

With reference to *Sir Amadas*, two points of special interest appear. The hero is provided the wherewithal for his successful courtship by means of a wreck to which he is directed by the White Knight; and he is required to divide his child as well as his wife with his helper. These peculiarities, together with the different opening, make it improbable that *Richars*, as preserved, was the direct source of the romance, though its author may have known some text either of that romance, or of *Lion de Bourges*. It seems more likely, however, that the source of *Sir Amadas* was rather the common original of both those versions. In the present state of the evidence it is impossible to do more than to show, as I have attempted to do, that the fourteenth-century *Sir Amadas* is a member of the little group under discussion.

The proposed division of the son is peculiarly important in that it connects the group with the stories in which *The Grateful Dead* is compounded with the theme of *Amis and Amiloun*. Indeed, the general relationship of *The Spendthrift Knight* to that theme must be considered in a later chapter [1] after more important compounds have been

[1] See chapter vii.

discussed. It will be noted that the group just considered is purely literary and purely mediaeval. Though it has representatives in Italy, Germany, Sweden, and England, it is to all intents and purposes French in source and character. Five of its members are the only variants treated in this chapter where the question of dividing the hero's prize is brought up. The group thus stands by itself, and may be considered as an entity when we come to a discussion of the larger matters of relationship.

A solitary folk-tale now demands attention—my *Breton II*. The Grateful Dead in a simple form is here combined with a story told of Gregory the Great,[1] as Luzel, to whom the tale was recounted by a *Breton* peasant, indeed briefly noted.[2] The Breton tale runs as follows: A rich lord and lady had no children. While the lady was praying to St. Peter in a chapel that was being repaired, she fell a victim to a young painter, and had by him a son, who was named after St. Peter. When the boy was twelve years of age, he carried St. Peter across a stream one day, while his shepherd companion

---

[1] The *Trentall of St. Gregory.* The Old French text has been edited by P. Meyer, *Romania*, xv. 281-283. The English versions, of which the first seems to be taken from this, are found in the following MSS.: (A) Vernon MS. fol. 230, ed. Horstmann, *Engl. Stud.* viii. 275-277, and *The Minor Poems of the Vernon MS.* i., E.E.T.S. 98, 1892, pp. 260-268; Vernon MS. fol. 303, variants given in Horstmann's ed. for E.E.T.S.; MS. Cotton Caligula A II., ed. Furnivall, *Political, Religious, and Love Poems*, E.E.T.S. 15, 1866, pp. 83-92, reprinted by Horstmann, E.E.T.S. pp. 260-268; MS. Lambeth 306, variants given by Furnivall; a critical text with variants of the four was made by A. Kaufmann, *Trentalle Sancti Gregorii, Erlanger Beiträge*, iii. 29-44, 1889. (B) MS. 19, 3, 1, Advocates' Libr., Edinburgh, ed. Turnbull, *The Visions of Tundale*, 1843, pp. 77 ff., and Bülbring, *Anglia*, xiii. 301-308; MS. Kk. I, 6, Camb. Univ. Libr., ed. Kaufmann, pp. 44-49. Kaufmann in his introduction discusses the relations of the versions. See further Varnhagen, *Anglia*, xiii. 105 f. Another legend of Gregory in popular fiction is treated by Bruce in his edition of *De Ortu Waluuanii, Publications Mod. Lang. Ass.* xiii. 372-377. The story in the *Gesta Romanorum* to which Luzel, i. 83, note, refers is this rather than our tale.

[2] i. 83 and 90, notes.

carried Christ. The companion died soon after. Pierre then set forth to visit his patron in Paradise. On his way he stopped overnight at the house of an old woman, whose husband lay unburied because there was no money to pay the priest. Pierre gave all his money for the interment, and went on. When he came to the sea, a naked man, who said that he was the dead, carried him across to a point near the gates of Paradise. There he found Peter, and was shown the glories of heaven by the Saviour, as well as Purgatory and Hell. In the last he saw a chair reserved for his mother, but by his entreaties induced the Lord to grant her a release on condition of doing penance himself for her. So he was told to put on a spiked girdle, to throw the key of it into the sea, and not to take it off till the key should be found. After donning this instrument Pierre was carried by the ghost back to his own land, where he lived on alms—first on the public ways, and later, without discovering himself, in his father's castle. During his father's absence he was killed at the command of his mother, but was dug up alive by his father and treated with respect. One day at a feast he found the key in the head of a fish. When the girdle was opened, he died, and his soul was borne to heaven by angels.

Two Danish variants present a curious but not inexplicable combination of *The Grateful Dead* with *Puss in Boots*, as was noted by Köhler.[1] *Danish I.* relates how a youth pays three marks, which is his all, to bury the body of a dead man, for whose interment the priest has demanded payment in advance. He is then joined by another youth, who is the ghost of the dead, and goes to a certain city. There, by giving himself out as a prince at the advice of his companion, who provides him with proper trappings, he wins the hand of a princess. In *Danish II.* an old soldier pays his last three marks to

---

[1] *Or. und Occ.* iii. 99 f.

prevent three creditors from digging up a corpse. He is joined by a pale stranger, who takes him in a leaden ship to a land where he marries a princess, who is fated to marry no one save a man who comes in this way. The stranger secures, by a lying ruse, a troll's castle for the hero, and, after explaining that he is the ghost of the buried debtor, disappears.

The traces of the *Puss in Boots* motive[1] are, I think, sufficiently clear, especially in the first of the two variants, since the point of that familiar tale is certainly that the hero marries a woman of high estate by making himself out as of equal rank, substantiating his statements by a succession of clever ruses. That the grateful dead enables him to fulfil the required conditions is an introduction that could easily replace the ordinary one, especially since a helper of some sort is necessary to the story. Just what the relation of these two variants is to other *Puss in Boots* stories does not here concern us. From the side of *The Grateful Dead*, however, it is possible to see how the combination—found only in two folk-tales from a single country, it will be observed—may have arisen. The benefits bestowed on the hero show an essential likeness to those found in a widespread compound type to be studied in a later chapter,[2] where the thankful dead helps his friend to obtain a wife by the performance of some feat. Since the combination now in consideration seems to be confined to the region about Denmark, while mediaeval and modern examples of the other are found in many lands, it may be regarded as a mere variation on the better-known compound type, produced by the similarity of the two endings. Yet

---

[1] See *Das Märchen vom gestiefelten Kater*, Leipzig, 1843; Benfey, *Pantschatantra*, i. 222; Grimm, *Kinder- und Hausmärchen*, iii. 288; Liebrecht, *Dunlop's Geschichte der Prosadichtungen*, 1851, p. 286; Polívka, *Arch. f. slav. Phil.* xix. 248; etc.

[2] Chapter vi.

it has to be treated separately, because it involves an independent theme.

An echo of the simple theme of *The Grateful Dead* is found in two English plays—Massinger's *Fatal Dowry* and Rowe's *Fair Penitent.* In the former young Charalois goes to prison to release his father's body from the clutch of creditors, who wish to keep it unburied for vengeance.[1] He is rescued by Rochfort, who pays the debts and gives him his daughter in marriage. The intrigues of love and vengeance that follow do not concern us. In Rowe's play, which was based on Massinger's, this part has been curtailed to a few slight references. Altamont gives himself as ransom for his father's body to the greedy creditors, who will not allow burial to take place. He is rewarded by the care and bounty of Sciolto, who becomes a second father to him.

Stephens was certainly right in connecting[2] the story in *The Fatal Dowry* with *The Grateful Dead,* though it is only a fragment and lacks some of the most essential features of the complete theme. The ghost, indeed, does not appear at all, but the part played by Rochfort may be regarded as a greatly sophisticated reminiscence of that trait, especially since he not only rescues the hero, but provides him with a wife. The echo of the theme is too vague for us to distinguish the form in which it was found by Massinger, though I think that we should not go far wrong in supposing that he had in mind some narrative, either popular or literary, nearly approaching the compound type treated in chapter vi. below. As one of the comparatively few traces that the motive has left in England this double dramatic use is not without interest.[3]

---

[1] An unnecessarily nauseating reason is given by one of them (Act i. sc. i.), but this seems to be of Massinger's invention.

[2] P. 8.

[3] It is interesting also to note that a Viennese dramatist of our own day has adapted Massinger's drama, retaining a vague reminiscence of the thankful dead. The curious may see *Der Graf von Charolais* by Richard Beer-Hofmann, 1905.

CHAPTER IV.

THE GRATEFUL DEAD AND THE POISON MAIDEN.

ONE of the most prevalent types of *The Grateful Dead* is that in which it has combined with *The Poison Maiden*, a theme almost world-wide in distribution and application. From the time of Benfey and Stephens[1] the connection between the two themes has been regarded as vital. Though Hippe recognised that the stories were perhaps originally independent,[2] he took the compound as his point of departure and derived all other forms from it. As will be seen in the course of our study, such a filiation is exceedingly improbable, if the essential features of *The Grateful Dead* and *The Poison Maiden* be closely examined. Hippe went wrong, I should say, in failing to differentiate between what traits belong to the former and what to the latter theme.

As a matter of fact, *The Poison Maiden* exists in a cycle of its own. Any doubt about this and any necessity of studying the theme in detail here is removed by the valuable monograph of Wilhelm Hertz, *Die Sage vom Giftmädchen*,[3] in which the literature of the subject has been marshalled with masterly skill. Starting with the

---

[1] See pp. 1 and 2.   [2] P. 181.

[3] *Abhandlungen der k. bayerischen Akademie der Wissenschaften*, 1893, pp. 89-166. Reprinted, with some additional notes by the editor, in *Gesammelte Abhandlungen von Wilhelm Hertz*, ed. F. von der Leyen, 1905, pp. 156-277.

stories of how a maiden, who had been fed with snake-poison, was sent to Alexander the Great from India by an enemy, and how the plot to kill the emperor through her embraces was foiled by the cunning of Aristotle,[1] Hertz shows[2] that the central idea of the tale is the belief that a man could be killed by sexual connection with a woman who had been nourished on poison. In most of the variants, to be sure, it is the bite of the woman that is venomous, while in others it is her glance or her breath; but these are natural modifications. Without following the study into details, the important fact to remember is that there has existed from early times a tale relating how a man was saved by a watchful friend on his bridal night from a maiden whose embraces were certain death.[3] With this in mind we can safely proceed to a consideration of the variants of *The Grateful Dead* which have similar features.

Twenty-four of the stories in my list fall into this category, viz.: *Tobit, Armenian, Gypsy, Siberian, Russian*

[1] The existing versions go back to the pseudo-Aristotelian *De secretis secretorum* or *De regimine principum*, which was taken from the Arabic in the twelfth century (Hertz, p. 92). It is probable, however, that the tale existed far earlier than this and came from India (Hertz, pp. 151-155).

[2] Pp. 115 ff.

[3] Two Asiatic parallels not cited by Hertz will serve to illustrate the theme further. One of these is "The Story of Swet-Basanta" from Lal Behari Day, *Folk-tales of Bengal*, 1883, pp. 100 f. The hero is found by an elephant and made king of a land, where the successive sovereigns are killed every night mysteriously. He watches and sees something like a thread coming from the queen's nostrils. This proves to be a great serpent, which he kills, thus remaining as king. The other is from J. H. Knowles, *Folk-tales of Kashmir*, 1888, pp. 32 ff., "A Lach of Rupees for a Bit of Advice." A prince pays a lach of rupees for a paper containing four rules of conduct. His father exiles him for this extravagance. In his wanderings the prince finds a potter alternately laughing and crying because his son must soon marry a princess, who has to be wedded anew each night. So the prince marries the woman instead and kills two serpents that come from her nostrils, thus retaining the kingdom. In these two stories there is no question of aid coming to the hero; he is saved by his own watchfulness.

I., II., III., and *IV., Servian II., III.,* and *IV., Bulgarian, Esthonian II., Finnish, Rumanian I., Irish I., II.,* and *III., Breton I., Danish III., Norwegian II., Simrock X., Harz I., Jack the Giant Killer,* and *Old Wives' Tale.* All but three of them [1] are folk-tales, a fact that considerably simplifies the discussion.

According to the apocryphal story, Tobit buries by night the dead who lie in the street. He is thrown into prison, and later becomes blind and poverty-stricken. He sends his son Tobias to his brother Gabael for the return of a loan. The youth is accompanied by the angel Raphael in disguise, who calls himself Azarias. On the journey Tobias catches a fish and preserves the heart, liver, and gall at the bidding of his companion. When they arrive at their journey's end, the angel, as go-between, asks Gabael's daughter Sara in wedlock for Tobias, though seven men have died while consummating their marriage with her. By burning the heart and liver of the fish at the command of the angel, and by prayer, Tobias escapes; for the demon Asmodeus is driven out of the maiden and bound by Raphael. With his bride and companion Tobias goes home, where he cures Tobit's blindness by means of the gall of the fish. After being offered half of the wealth that he has brought the family, Raphael explains his identity and disappears.

This variant is peculiar in that the father does the good action, while the son is chiefly rewarded. Indeed, it is the son whose life is saved from the possessed woman whom he marries. Moreover, the grateful dead is replaced by an angel, who indeed commends Tobit for his good deed, but is certainly a substitute for the ghost. Obviously *Tobit* with such peculiarities as these cannot be regarded as the general source of the wide-spread folk-tale. At the same time we must not forget that it has been, perhaps, the best-loved story in the

---

[1] *Tobit, Danish III.* (Andersen's tale), and Peele's *Old Wives' Tale.*

Apocrypha,[1] and that its influence on details of the narrative may be looked for almost anywhere in Christendom.

In the *Armenian* story from Transcaucasia [2] a man finds a corpse hanging in a tree and being beaten by his late creditors. The man pays the debt and buries the body. Some years later he becomes poor. A rich man offers him in marriage his daughter, with whom five bridegrooms have already met death on the wedding night. While thinking over the proposition, he is approached by a man who offers to become his servant for half of his future possessions, and counsels him to marry the woman. On the night of the marriage the servant stands with a sword in the chamber, cuts off the head of a serpent that comes from the bride's mouth, and pulls out its body. Later he asks for his share of his master's gains. When he is about to split the woman through the middle, a second snake glides from her mouth. The servant then says that he is the ghost of the corpse long ago rescued, and disappears. Here the story appears in a very normal form, except that the hero is not taking a journey at the time of his kind deed, and that he waits several years for his reward. Moreover, the second snake appears to be due to reduplication.

In *Gypsy* a youth gives his last twelve piasters for the release of a corpse, which is being maltreated by Jews. The ghost of the dead man follows him and promises to get him a bride if he will share her with him. The youth consents and marries a woman whose five bridegrooms have died on the wedding night. The companion keeps watch in the chamber and cuts off the head of a dragon that comes from the bride's mouth.

---

[1] For example, it appears in Schischmánoff's *Légendes religieuses bulgares*, 1896, pp. 194-201, side by side with our *Bulgarian* tale.

[2] I summarise from Köhler's reprint in *Germania*, iii. pp. 202 ff.

Later he demands his half of the woman, and takes a sword to cut her asunder, when she screams and disgorges the dragon's body. The ghost then explains the situation and disappears.[1]

With the *Siberian* variant some very important modifications enter. A soldier buys a picture of the Saviour from a peasant and maltreats it. A merchant's son then buys it out of reverence and takes it to his mother. Later he helps an old man on a raft and goes with him to market. There he meets the daughter of a priest and, by the advice of his friend, marries her. When the old man strikes her with a whip, she splits open, and the devil comes out. She is put together again by the mysterious companion, and accompanies them home, where the old man asks for a division of the gains they have made together. Again he divides the woman. After she has been burned, she is found living and purified. Then the old man says that he is God and departs.

This tale, found among the Turkish race of southern Siberia, has transformed the opening incident altogether. For the burial of the corpse it substitutes a good deed, which is entirely different from the original trait. Yet it is evident that we have to do with *The Grateful Dead*, after all, since the divine image is rescued from senseless contumely and God himself appears in the rôle of the thankful ghost. It is evident also that the theme is combined with *The Poison Maiden*. Though we do not hear of any misadventures of other men with the priest's daughter, the marvels which attend her purification indicate the danger in which the hero stood.

Russian I. is likewise peculiar in several respects. The younger of two brothers angers his parents by going

---

[1] Paspati's tale on pp. 605 ff. also has a dragon slain on a wedding night by a youth, who keeps watch. This single trait in a totally different setting must be borrowed from a Gypsy form of the simple or compound theme.

to the wars without their permission. He is killed. Later he appears to his brother, asking him to implore pardon of their mother, whose anger prevents him from resting quietly in his grave. The elder brother thus succeeds in giving peace to the ghost. Later, when he marries a merchant's daughter, whose first two husbands have been killed by a dragon on the wedding night, he is saved by the ghost of the dead, which keeps watch in the chamber with a sword and kills the nine-headed dragon.

This tale stands almost alone [1] in giving the two chief characters personal relations, since it is nearly always a total stranger whom the hero benefits. That actual burial of the dead does not come in question is not so remarkable, as various changes have been made in this trait. One story,[2] indeed, which otherwise has no likeness, similarly makes the dead man uneasy in his grave. The beginning of *Russian I.* has thus suffered considerable modification. The ending is also different from the normal type in that the division of the property and the woman has entirely disappeared.

Russian II. has also some peculiarities, though none which is difficult to explain. A youth named Hans receives three hundred rubles from his uncle, who has taken his inheritance, and goes into the world. In another province he ransoms with his whole stock of money an unbeliever, who is being bled by the people. He has the poor man baptised, but is not able to save his life, so sorely has he been wounded. The people, however, pay for proper burial. Hans goes on and is joined by an angel, who proposes that he take him as uncle and divide with him whatever they get while in one another's company. They come to a city where

---

[1] See *Annamite*, *Greek*, *Oliver*, and *Walewein*. There is something approaching it in *Rumanian I.*

[2] *Icelandic I.*

the king proposes that Hans marry his daughter, and
to this the hero agrees at his companion's advice, despite
the protests of the citizens, who say that the princess has
already strangled six bridegrooms. On the wedding
night the uncle keeps watch, and slays a dragon which
is approaching to kill the young man. After two months
the pair set out for home with the uncle. On the way
they are saved by the old man from robbers, and get a
store of gold. When they arrive at the place where the
uncle first appeared, he calls for a fulfilment of their
agreement, and saws the bride asunder. Young dragons
come out of her; but, when she has been washed and
sprinkled with water, she is made whole. The angel
thereupon parts with the couple.

For the burial of the dead we have in this tale the
interesting substitution of an unsuccessful attempt of the
hero to save a man's life by paying his entire inheritance
as ransom. That the man dies and is buried shows how
the change probably arose, Strangely enough, as in the
case of *Tobit*, an angel appears in the rôle of the grateful
dead, and, even more oddly, takes the form of the hero's
uncle, who gave him the money with which he set forth
on his journey. The recurrence of the angel in this and
in one other variant[1] inclines me to the belief that the
essential feature of the reward in the original story was
that it came from heaven. The remainder of *Russian II.*
has no characteristic unusual in the tales where the
woman is actually divided to get rid of the snakes or
dragons.

In *Russian III.*[2] the youngest of three brothers rescues
a swimming coffin from the sea and takes it on his ship.
From the coffin comes a man clothed in a white shirt,
who enters the service of his rescuer, and helps him win
a beautiful princess as wife. A six-headed dragon has
hitherto killed all her bridegrooms on the wedding night,

[1] *Simrock IV.*   [2] See Hippe, p. 145.

but it is overcome by the hero through his obedience to the advice of his servant. The latter cleanses the bride's body of the dragon brood and goes away. Here the opening has been modified, though not beyond recognition, since the rescued man is clearly enough the grateful dead.

Russian IV., taken like the preceding from a folk-book, differs from that in only minor points, though the ampler form in which I have found it makes it of more importance. The three sons of a czar go out in separate ships to see the world. The youngest, named Sila, rescues a swimming coffin, which his brothers have not heeded, and buries it on shore. There he leaves his companions, and goes on alone till joined by a man dressed in a shroud, who says that he is the rescued corpse and proposes that Sila win a certain Princess Truda as wife by his aid. The hero is dismayed when he sees the walls of her city decorated with the heads of countless former suitors, but he is told by his servant not to fear. On the bridal night he is counselled to keep silence, and, when his wife presses her hand on his breast, to beat her, as she is in league with a six-headed dragon. Sila obeys, the dragon appears, and the servant cuts off two of its heads. Two more heads are cut off on the second night, and the remaining two on the third. The bride is not completely cleansed, however, till the end of a year, when the servant cuts her in two, burns the evil things that emerge from her body, and sprinkles her with living water to make her well again. He then disappears.

Here the grateful dead appears with perfect clearness, as he did not in *Russian III.* The course of events by which the lady is won does not differ materially from that of *Russian II.* Presumably *III.* would follow the same procedure, had we an adequate summary. *III.* and *IV.* are like *I.*, and different from *II.*, in omitting all mention of any division of property or of the woman between hero and assistant. The division for the sake of cleansing in *IV.* is, however, actual.

Not without contamination from another source, *Russian V.* and *VI.* still belong to the class containing variants with *The Poison Maiden.* In *Russian V.* the only son of a rich man went out into the world to seek his fortune. On the road he gave a large sum of money for two horses. Later he stopped at an inn, where the widow of the landlord was weeping because she had no money to pay the debts of her husband, who was cursed by all the people, though he had been dead two years. The hero gave all his money to save the memory of the dead man, and proceeded. Soon he met two unsatisfied creditors, who still cursed the dead landlord, and to them he gave his two horses. Not long afterward he was joined by a man, who accompanied him on condition of receiving half of what they might win together. They came to a place where a lord offered a thousand rubles to anyone who would watch his daughter's corpse over night in a chapel. The hero undertook the adventure, and received payment in advance. At dark his companion came to him, and gave him a cross as protection. At midnight the lady came out of her coffin, but could not find the man because he held the cross. The same adventure was repeated the next night. On the third night the hero, according to his companion's advice, got into the coffin when the vampire rose, and would not get out for all her entreaties, being protected by the cross. So in the morning both were found alive, and were betrothed. Then came the companion, cut the maiden into halves, took out her entrails, and put her together again, when she became very beautiful. Next day he called the hero aside, explained his identity with the dead landlord, and disappeared.

Russian VI. differs from the above in several points,

but is closely allied to it. There were two brothers, one good and the other stingy. The former expended in benevolence all his wealth, save a hundred rubles, while the latter grew richer and richer. A poor man borrowed a hundred rubles from the miser, calling St. George as witness that he would pay; but he died in debt. The rich brother came to the widow, and said that he would get his money from St. George if not from the dead man. He pulled down an image of the saint from the wall, dug up the corpse, and spat upon them both. At this juncture the good brother came by, and gave his last hundred rubles to put the matter right. He then went to a large city, where the king's daughter had eaten all the deacons who watched with her dead body. So when volunteers were called for to stay with her, the hero offered to undertake the task at the advice of an old man, who promised to pray for his safety on condition of receiving half his winnings. He received payment in advance from the king, and divided with the old man, by whom he was given a sanctified coal, a taper, a cross, and a scapulary, together with advice how to act. So he entered the chapel, lighted his taper, closed his eyes, made the sign of the cross, and enclosed himself in a circle marked with the coal near the head of the bier. At cockcrow the vampire came out all blue and grinning; but, though she yelled horribly, she could not touch the man in the circle, who put the cross in the coffin. At the second cockcrow she tried to get into the coffin, and unavailingly begged him to take out the cross. At the third cockcrow he put the scapulary on her, whereupon she rose and thanked him, promising to be his wife and servant. So in the morning the hero married her and received the kingdom from her father. To their chamber that night came the old man, and recalled the agreement to divide. He cut the lady into halves, minced her flesh on the table, and blew on the bits, whereupon she came together more beautiful than ever. The helper then threw off his gaberdine, and showed himself to be St. George.

In the two stories just summarized *The Grateful Dead* is clear enough, though in *VI.* St. George has ousted the ghost from part of its proper functions, just as the angel does in *Tobit, Russian II.*, and *Simrock IV.*, God in *Siberian*, and various saints elsewhere. The introduction in *VI.* is a unique trait, as far as I know. In both the variants the main features of the theme appear without distortion, including the picturesque cleansing of the woman by actual division. *The Poison Maiden*, however, has been replaced by a story of similar character, but of different content, which I have not elsewhere found compounded with *The Grateful Dead.* A vampire infests a church (or a churchyard). A soldier is sent to watch nights, and to try to dislodge her. He successfully counters her tricks, and finally gets hold of something belonging to her, which he refuses to return. Thereupon she is reduced to submission, promises him happiness, and is married to him with the consent of the king.[1] This tale, it will be evident, bears a strong likeness to *The Poison Maiden* in the figure of the

[1] References to this story have been collected by G. Polívka, and printed in *Archiv f. slav. Phil.* xix. 251, in citing our *Russian V.* He says : "Vgl. Романовъ, iv. S. 124, Nr. 65 ; Weryho, *Pod. białoruskie*, S. 46 ; Худяковъ, i. Nr. 11, 12 ; Садовниковъ, S. 44, 310 ; Манжура, 61 ; Драгомановъ Малор. Преп, S. 268 f. ; Dowojna Sylwestrowicz, ii. 129 f. ; Karłowicz, Nr. 19 ; Kolberg, viii. S. 138 f., Nr. 55, 56 ; xiv. S. 72 f., Nr. 16, 17 ; Ciszewski, i. Nr. 128 ; Kulda, iii. Nr. 14 ; Strohal, Nr. 18, 19 ; Kres, iv. S. 350, Nr. 19 ; Th. Vernaleken, *Oesterr. K.H.M.* S. 44 f. ; Ul. Jahn, i. 92, 356 ; Pröhle, *Märchen für die Jugend*, S. 42 ; Wolf, *D.H.M.* 258 f. ; Sébillot, *Contes des marins*, S. 38." As far as I have been able to ascertain, these references are all to the tale sketched above, uncompounded with *The Grateful Dead.* I must thank Professor Wiener for my knowledge of the Slavic forms, which he very generously examined for me as far as the books were available, *viz.* Romanov, Khudyakov, Sadovnikov, Manžura, Dragomanov, Sylwestrowicz, and Kolberg.

heroine, though it certainly is independent. The vital difference between the two is the absence of any helping friend in the story of the vampire. Because of the lack of this figure it seems improbable that the tale was compounded with *The Grateful Dead* without the intermediary stage in which *The Poison Maiden* appears. I regard the vampire as usurping the place of the possessed maiden, and the two Russian variants as a secondary growth. Given the normal form of the compound as it appears in *Russian II.*, for instance, there would be no difficulty in substituting an even more gruesome figure for that of the heroine there depicted, and in making the hero's danger lie in a prenuptial attack on her part.

The three Servian tales, which fall in this section, differ widely in their characteristics. The first of them, *Servian II.*,[1] is the most nearly normal. Vlatko goes into the world to trade, but pays all his money to free from debt a corpse, which creditors are digging up in order to vent their spite upon it. He returns home, and is sent out again by his parents, receiving a greater sum of money and, from his mother, an apple by means of which he can tell the intentions of anyone who desires his friendship by the way.[2] He is joined by a man, who cuts the apple into two exact halves, and so is accepted as a friend. After Vlatko has prospered in trade, the friend proposes that he marry the emperor's daughter, with whom ninety-nine men have already died on the wedding night. Arrangements are made, and the friend keeps watch in the bridal chamber. During the night he cuts off the heads of three snakes, which come from the lady's mouth. Sometime afterwards all three set out for Vlatko's home; and on the way the hero divides his property with his friend.

[1] See Hippe, pp. 145 f.

[2] For the test of friendship with an apple, see Köhler's notes in Gonzenbach, *Sicil. Märchen*, ii. 259 f., and in *Arch. f. slav. Phil.* v. 44 ff.

Jestingly the latter proposes that they divide the wife, and, after blindfolding the husband, shakes her three times, when three dead snakes come out of her. Thereupon he disappears.

Like *Armenian* and *Gypsy*, this variant has the ghost cut off the head of the monster (here three snakes) that possesses the maiden. The actual division of the woman as it appears in those tales occurs here as a mere jest, which is the case with most of the European versions.[1]

Servian III. has a more romantic character. The daughter of an emperor had been married thirteen times, but each of her bridegrooms had died on the wedding night. A certain prince, who had fallen in love with her through a dream, set out for her castle. On the way he paid the debts of a poor man, whose corpse was held by creditors, and buried him. Soon after, he was met by a man who became his servant, and won a castle for him by a wonderful adventure. After the wedding this man killed the snakes that came out of the bride, and also caused her to disgorge three snake eggs by threatening her with his drawn sword. He then disappeared.

This variant shows traces of foreign substance in the dream and the winning of the castle by the unrevealed companion. Possibly the latter trait unites it with the combined type of which *The Water of Life* is one of the elements. It will be noticed that the division of the property and of the woman is not brought into question, though the sword is used somewhat incongruously for the removal of the last traces of the heroine's snaky infestation. Thus, by an evident change in structure,

---

[1] Hippe is in error, however, when he says (p. 178) that the division is everywhere modified in the European variants. See *Russian II., IV., V.* and *VI., Bulgarian*, and *Esthonian II.* Moreover, I believe that Hippe's theory puts the cart before the horse—that the actual division is not so ancient a trait as it seems. See pp. 74, 75 below.

the identity of the hero's companion is never explained.

With *Servian IV.*[1] we encounter a most serious problem, which must receive special treatment later on,[2]— the relation of *The Grateful Dead* to *The Thankful Beasts* theme. A poor youth three times set free a gold-fish which he had three times caught. Later he was cast out of his father's house and sent into the world. He was joined by a man, who swore friendship with him on a sword, and accompanied him to a city where many men had been mysteriously slain while undertaking to pass a night with the king's daughter. The hero undertook the adventure, and was saved by his companion, who cut off the head of a serpent that came from the princess's mouth. In the morning the youth was married to the lady, and divided all his property with his helper. On their way home the latter demanded half of the bride, and, while she was held by two servants, swung a sword above her. With a shriek she cast first two sections, and finally the tail, of a serpent from her mouth. Thereupon the friend leaped into the sea, for he was the gold-fish.

The burial of the dead has here been ousted by a good deed which the hero does to a gold-fish. That the trait is foreign to the type, however, seems clear. From the time when the companion appears to the hero, the story follows the normal course until the very end, when the man unexpectedly leaps into the sea. The thankful dead has been replaced by the thankful beast, but the tale really belongs to the present category, since otherwise it has all the characteristics of the type. Thus the division of the woman is almost precisely similar to that of *Armenian* and *Gypsy*—that is, the sword is raised, and the woman disgorges the serpent with a scream. That it comes out piecemeal may be a faulty recollection

[1] See Hippe, p. 146. [2] See chapter vii.

of the actual division. As so often, it is not stated that the companion made a share of the gains a condition of his help.

Bulgarian is in some respects very primitive, though fragmentary. A father sends his son out into the world to gain experience. The youth is joined by an archangel, who promises him assistance on condition that he will pay their joint expenses and will be obedient. The companion kills a negro and a serpent, and goes with the hero into their den, where the adventurers find, but leave, great treasure. They come to a city where the king's daughter has been thrice married, each time only to have her bridegroom die on the wedding night. Now she is to be given to any man who can live with her one night; and many wooers have died in the attempt. The youth offers himself as a suitor, and is saved by the archangel, who draws a serpent out of the woman. Later he helps the hero to get the wealth previously found in the cave, and demands the division of everything, even the wife. When he cuts her in two, many little snakes fall out of her body. He then unites her, and gives the hero all the riches they have obtained.

The burial of the dead has entirely disappeared, as will be observed, though the other traits of the story show that we must regard it as of the type now under consideration. The appearance of the archangel as companion, and the plunder which they take by the way, suggest the influence of *Tobit*, which indeed appears as a folk-tale in the same collection.[1] The conditions made by the angel are only slightly altered from the normal form, while every other feature is found intact, even to the actual division of the woman.

Esthonian II. has altogether lost the essential features of our theme; and it has besides put in several traits from a *märchen*, which, as we shall soon see, is joined

[1] See p. 47, note, above.

to ours with considerable frequency. The inclusion of this variant here is justified only by some vague traces indicating that the extraneous parts of the narrative have replaced others which, if preserved, would make it an ordinary representative of *The Grateful Dead.*

A certain couple had a weak-minded son, who could not learn. Wishing to get rid of him, the father took the boy into a forest and gave him gladly to an old man whom he chanced to meet. From the man the youth received books in foreign tongues, which he learned to read in a day. He then wandered till he came to a city, where lived a princess who was in the power of devils and went to church with them every night. The hero watched in the church for three nights, with three, six, and twelve candles, successively. Thus on the third night he freed the princess and married her, receiving half the kingdom. He then sought the old man, who told him to cut the woman in halves and divide her. The old man halved her himself, when there sprang out a serpent, a toad, and a lizard. After this he gave her back to her husband.

The obscurity of motivation in this tale makes apparent the extensive revision that it has undergone. The introduction is nowhere else found combined, as far as I know, with the stories of our cycle. The characteristics of *The Poison Maiden* are sufficiently evident in the conclusion; but there seems to be no way to account for the peculiar form of demonic possession, together with the actual division of the woman, except by supposing, with Dutz,[1] that the variant has lost the part concerning the burial of the dead man. If this be true, the story belongs in the category where it is here placed.

The *Finnish* variant[2] presents difficulties of a somewhat different sort. A merchant's son, to whom it has been foretold that he will marry a three-horned maiden,

---

[1] P. 19.   [2] See Hippe, pp. 148 f.

goes abroad to escape this fate. There he sees the corpse of a debtor hanging nailed to a church wall, and insulted by the passers-by. He expends all but nine silver kopecks in rescuing the body, and turns homeward. He is joined by a companion, who makes the money last three days, and on the fourth arranges for him to marry the three-horned daughter of a king. On the wedding night the helper brings the hero fresh-cut twigs. By beating the maiden with these her blood is purified, the horns drop off, and she becomes very beautiful.

No new material is here introduced ; but the handling is considerably changed, and the narrative abridged. The woman in the case is three-horned instead of possessed by snakes, nor is there any hint of harm to the bridegroom. A reminiscence of the division of the woman, though not of the dowry, appears in the beating which the ghostly companion gives her, whereby she is freed from her horns and made very beautiful. The variant appears to be weakened by frequent retelling.

Rumanian I. is more striking, since it has undergone both revision and addition. The only daughter of an emperor wears out twelve pairs of slippers every night, until her father offers her hand and the heirship of the kingdom to any man who can explain this extraordinary and costly habit. Many men of high birth and low make the attempt unsuccessfully. Meanwhile, a certain peasant, whose servant had died when his year of service was but half ended, had placed the body in a chest under the roof in revenge for his disappointment. The new servant had discovered this, and had given the corpse the rites due the dead, as far as permitted by his master. When he departs at the end of his year of service, the dead man comes from the earth, thanks him, and proposes that they swear on the cross to be brothers. So they do, and go on together till they come to an iron wood. The vampire breaks off a twig, and casts it to the earth in the place where the emperor's daughter comes at night with the sons of the dragon. When she appears, she sees the broken twig, and is afraid. So she goes to the copper wood, where she sees another twig broken by the vampire, and hastens on to the place where the sons of the dragon dwell. It is in going so far that she wears out her slippers. When she comes to the place, and is about to sit down at table, she drops her handkerchief. The vampire, who has followed her from the copper wood in the form of a cat, takes it away, as he does also the spoon that falls from her hand and the ring that falls from her finger. He goes back to the copper wood with them, and explains everything to his friend. The latter takes them to the emperor and wins the lady.

This curious tale has several elements which make it difficult to classify. As far as the kindness to the dead goes, the matter is simple. Instead of an agreement between the companions to divide their gains, however, an oath of brotherhood is introduced. This is probably a local substitution, since it has long been a custom of the Slavs of the south to swear brotherhood on the cross,[1] but it necessitates the further loss of important features at the end of the narrative such as the saving of the bridegroom on the wedding night and the division of the maiden (or some modification of that feature) by the vampire. Indeed, the heroine is rather enchanted than possessed. The whole series of acts by which she is freed introduces traits into the narrative which we have hitherto met only in *Esthonian II.* Were it not that they are repeated in all the other members of the group save *Breton I.*, which we have still to consider, there would be considerable doubt about placing

---

[1] See note by Schott, p. 473, in which he gives evidence based on personal knowledge, and Grimm, *Geschichte der deutschen Sprache*, p. 92. I have touched on the matter in *Engl. Stud.* xxxvi. 195-201.

this variant under the category of *The Grateful Dead + The Poison Maiden.* As it is, we can with security say that this and the following versions belong here. They have simply modified the normal form by the addition of certain elements from another theme.

The three Irish versions all have this form. In *Irish I.* a king's son, while hunting, pays five pounds to the creditors of a dead man, so that he may be buried. Later the prince kills a raven, and declares that he will marry only that woman who has hair as black as the raven, skin as white as snow, and cheeks as red as blood upon the snow.[1] On his way to find her he meets a red-haired youth, who takes service with him for half of what they may gain in a year and a day. The youth obtains for him from various giants by threats of what his master will do[2] horses of gold and silver, a sword of light, a cloak of darkness, and the slippery shoes. When they come to the castle of the maiden, he helps the Prince to keep over night a comb and a pair of scissors in spite of enchantment, and he obtains at her bidding the lips of the giant enchanter, which are the last that she has kissed. He then tells the prince and the maiden's father to strike her three times, when three devils come from her mouth in fire. So the prince marries her, and is ready at the end of a year and a day to divide his child[3] at the servant's command. But the latter explains that he is the soul of the dead man, and disappears.

Irish II. differs little except in details from the above. The king of Ireland's son sets forth to find a woman with hair as black as the raven, skin as white as snow,

---

[1] This trait is found not infrequently in other settings. See, for example, Vernaleken, *Oesterreichische Kinder- und Hausmärchen*, p. 141.

[2] This trait recalls *Puss in Boots*, which is otherwise compounded with *The Grateful Dead*. See preceding chapter, p. 42, and p. 70 below.

[3] See chapter vii.

and cheeks as red as blood. Ten pounds of the twenty
which he takes with him he pays to release the corpse
of a man on which writs are laid. He meets a short
green man, who goes with him for his wife's first kiss ;
and he comes upon a gunner, a man listening to the grow-
ing grass, a swift runner, a man blowing a windmill with one
nostril, and a strong man, all of whom accompany him for
the promise of a house and garden apiece. After various
adventures in the castles of giants, they arrive in the
east, where the prince's lady dwells. She says that her
suitor must loose her *geasa* from her before she can marry
him. With the help of the short green man he gives
her the scissors, the comb, and the King of Porson's
head, which she requires. He is then told to get three
bottles of healing water from the well of the western
world. The runner sets out for them, and is stopped
and put to sleep by an old hag on the way back ; but
the earman hears him snoring, the gunman sees him and
wakes him up, and the windman keeps the hag back
till he returns. Finally the strong man crushes three
miles of steel needles so that the prince can walk over
them. Thus the bride is won. The short green man
claims the first kiss, and finds her full of serpents, which
he picks out of her. He then tells the youth that he is
the man who was in the coffin, and disappears with his
fellows.

In *Irish III.* three brothers set out from home with
three pounds apiece. The youngest gives his all to pay
a dead man's debts to three giants. He shares his food
with a poor man, who offers to be his servant, saying
that the corpse was his brother, and had appeared to
him in a dream.[1] Jack the servant frightens the first
giant into giving up his sword of sharpness, the second
giant his cloak of darkness, and the third giant his shoes

[1] Kennedy says, p. 38 : "In some versions of 'Jack the Master,' etc.,
Jack the servant is the spirit of the dead man."

of swiftness. The two Jacks come to the castle of a king, whose daughter has to be wooed by accomplishing three tasks. Jack the servant follows the princess in the cloak of darkness to the demon king of Moróco and rescues her scissors. Next day Jack the master runs a race with the king and beats him because shod with the shoes of swiftness. That night Jack the servant goes again to the demon king and cuts off his head with the sword of sharpness, thus accomplishing the third task. So Jack the master marries the princess.

These three variants make evident the nature of the foreign material in *Esthonian II.* and *Rumanian I.* The whole sub-group, indeed, has in combination with *The Grateful Dead + The Poison Maiden* important elements from the themes of *The Water of Life* and *The Lady and the Monster.* These features will be considered in detail in a later chapter,[1] when we study the general type *The Grateful Dead + The Water of Life.* For the present it is enough to indicate how the addition has affected the type with which we are immediately concerned.

Of the three Irish tales, the first two have best preserved the characteristics of the compound as found in Asia and Eastern Europe. *Irish I.* has all the essential features of *Armenian* and *Gypsy,*—for example, the burial, the agreement to divide what is gained, and the removal of the evil things by which the woman is possessed. To be sure, the latter are devils, not serpents, and the woman is beaten, not divided. Yet the division appears in another form, since the hero is ready to share his child with the red-haired man, a trait connected with the theme of *Amis and Amiloun.*[2] *Irish II.* is in some respects more changed, and in some respects less, than *Irish I.* The agreement to divide is changed to a promise that the green man shall have the first kiss of

[1] Chapter vi.　　　　　　[2] See chapter vii.

the bride. On the other hand, the serpents in the woman's body are retained, a trait which is very primitive and very important in enabling us to identify the position of these variants. *Irish III.* has lost most of the typical features of the compound. Kennedy's evidence shows that Jack the servant is to be regarded as really the thankful dead ; but the agreement to divide the gains and the removal of the demons or serpents have entirely disappeared under pressure from the secondary theme, the essential idea of which is the accomplishment by the hero of certain unspelling tasks. In conjunction with the other two variants, however, the position of *Irish III.* is clear.

Very different from the Irish tales is *Breton I.*, since under the influence of a tendency very common in Brittany, the narrative has become a Mary legend and has lost its clearness of outline in the process. Yet it really belongs to this group, replacing by a dragon-fight and a rescue of the hero from the villain the cleansing of the bride. At least, I am led to the belief that such is the case by the fact that the story fits into no other category. Nor is it surprising that the position of the tale should be obscure in view of the grotesque transformation which it has undergone.

A youth named Mao pays all his money to have the body of a beggar interred. The spirit of the dead man helps him win the daughter of a rich man after killing a dragon in the stables. The lady's treacherous cousin tries to burn him alive in an old mill, whence he is saved by the ghost. He forgives the man, and is tricked into promising him half of all his possessions in order to save his wife. When a son is born, the villain demands its division. At the hero's appeal, the Virgin comes with the ghost and takes Mao and his family to heaven, while the cousin is sent to hell.

E

Norwegian II. and *Danish III.* stand together, since the relation of the latter (Andersen's *Reisekammeraten*) to the former is simply that of a literary redaction to its original. A brief analysis of each is, however, necessary.

In *Norwegian II.* a young peasant on account of a dream sets forth to win the hand of a princess. On his way he gives most of his money to bury a dishonest tapster, who has been executed and left frozen in a block of ice outside a church for passers-by to spit upon. As he proceeds, the youth is joined by the ghost of the tapster, who accompanies him. They go to a hill, where they get a magic sword from one witch, a golden ball of yarn from another, and a magical hat from a third. Of the yarn they make a bridge, and so come to the princess's castle. The hero is told to keep her scissors overnight and loses them ; but the companion rides behind the princess on her goat in the hat of invisibility, when she goes to her troll lover, and so rescues them. The hero is told to keep a golden ball overnight, and the same adventure is repeated. The hero is then told to bring what the princess is thinking of. The companion rides again with the princess and beats her with his sword, gets the troll's head for his master, and so enables him to win the lady. On the wedding night the hero flogs his wife at the advice of the companion, only just in time to save himself, indeed, as she is about to kill him with a butcher-knife. He dips her into a tub of whey, whence she comes out black as a raven, but after a rubbing with buttermilk and new milk she becomes very beautiful. The companion discovers his identity and disappears.

In *Danish III.* poor John, whose father has died, dreams of a beautiful princess, and sets forth to find her. He does various kind deeds by the way, and one night takes refuge from the storm in a church. There he sees two evil men dragging a corpse from its coffin, and pays his all that it may be buried. He is joined by the ghost of the dead man, who accompanies him. They get three rods from an old woman, who is healed by the comrade's salve, and they come to a city, where they get a sword from a showman, whose puppets are made alive by the salve. They come to a mountain, where the companion cuts off the wings of a great white swan and carries them along. They come at length to the city of the beautiful princess, who is a witch. Any-one can marry her who guesses three things, but every man who has tried has failed and been killed. John tells the king that he will try to win her, and is told to come the next day. In the night the comrade puts on the wings of the swan, takes the largest of the rods, and follows the princess when she flies out to the palace of her wizard lover. There he hears that she is to think of her shoe when her suitor comes in the morning. All the way to the mountain and back the comrade beats her so that the blood flows. The next morning he tells John to guess her shoe when asked what she has thought of. Everyone save the princess rejoices when the youth guesses right. The next night the companion beats the princess with two rods as she flies, and learns that she is to think of her glove. Again everyone is pleased with John's answer. The third night the companion takes all three rods and the sword. He cuts off the wizard's head when he learns that the princess is to think of that, and he gives it to John, wrapped in a handkerchief. John produces this when asked by the Princess what she has thought about, and so he wins her. That night, at the bidding of the com-panion, he dips her three times in a tub of water, into which have been shaken three swan's feathers and some drops from a flask. The first time she becomes a black swan, the second a white swan, and the third a more beautiful princess than ever. The next day the comrade explains his identity and disappears.

It will be seen that Andersen simply embroidered the Norwegian tale as was his wont, adding a good many picturesque details, and softening some features. The changes do not materially affect the course of the narrative, nor need they delay us here, interesting though they are of themselves,[1] since the position of the variant with reference to the story-type under consideration is perfectly clear. *Norwegian II.* demands further attention. Like *Esthonian II., Rumanian I.,* and *Irish I., II.,* and *III.,* it has the form *The Grateful Dead + The Poison Maiden + The Water of Life.* The burial of the dead is undisturbed, but the agreement between the companions to divide their gains has entirely disappeared, perhaps because the secondary theme takes so large a place. The removal of the poisonous habitants of the bride is clearly indicated, though it has been weakened into a flogging, which is given, however, only just in time to save the bridegroom from death. The subsequent milk bath seems to show a conflict between the conclusions of the two subsidiary motives—the end of *The Poison Maiden* being release from something like demonic possession, and that of *The Water of Life* in this form being release from a spell—though perhaps the bath is only a reduplication of the purifying process.

Simrock X. is not unlike the two variants just cited. A king's son wastes his property, and is sent out to shift for himself. He pays the debts of a naked corpse, and has only enough money left to pay his reckoning at his inn. So he takes the body to a wood, and buries it there. As he goes his way, he is met by a man, who becomes his follower and secures three rods, a sword, and a pair of wings from a dead raven. They come to

[1] The three rods with which the princess is flogged are found in *Harz I.* See pp. 69, 70 below.

a castle, where to win the king's daughter the prince has to guess her thoughts for three days in succession. The companion flies with her each night when she goes to her wizard for counsel, and learns that the prince must say "bread," "the princess's jewels," and "the wizard's head" in turn. On the last night he cuts off the wizard's head and brings it to his master, who displays it at court and so breaks the spell. When the couple are married, the companion explains that he is the spirit of the dead man, and disappears.

This variant obviously belongs to the same type as those preceding. As in *Irish I.* and *II.* the hero is a prince instead of a youth of low birth; but there is no general uniformity in this trait. The agreement of division and the violent dispossession of the heroine have disappeared. Indeed, so far has *The Water of Life* supplanted the other motives that the position of the tale is only evident when it is placed side by side with other versions of the same class. When so considered, however, the peculiar features of the succession of feats by which the bride is won appear very prominently, and establish the type.

Harz I. stands closer to *Norwegian II.* than the preceding. A youth pays his all for the burial of a poor man, whose ghost joins him. They go to a city, where a bespelled princess kills all her suitors who cannot answer a riddle. The companion spirit tells the youth to save her, explaining his own identity. He gives wings and an iron rod to the hero, who flies with the princess to a mountain spirit, and hears that he must guess that she is thinking of her father's white horse. The next night the youth follows her with two rods and is thus enabled to guess that she is thinking of her father's sword. The third night he follows her with two rods and a sword, with which he cuts off the monster's head. This he shows her in the morning when asked the usual question, and so he breaks the spell. On the wedding night he dips her thrice in water. The first time she comes from the bath a raven, the second time a dove, and the third time in her own shape, but purified.

The burial is here retained, but the agreement is entirely lost. Though the variant follows *Norwegian II.* in general, even to such details as the preliminary beating of the lady, and the bath of final purification, the important trait of flogging the bride, by which the hero is saved on the wedding night, has altogether disappeared. Like *Simrock X.*, the tale has obscured the first of the two secondary themes for the benefit of the second. Its position seems sure, however, as a member of the little group now being considered.

Jack the Giant-Killer clearly belongs to this group, approaching *Irish I.* in form. The earliest complete version that I know is unfortunately not older than the eighteenth century, and perhaps has lost several features of interest which might be found in earlier forms. King Arthur's son sets forth to free a lady possessed of seven spirits. At a market town in Wales he pays almost all his money to release the body of a man who died in debt. He gives his last twopence to an old woman, who meets him after he has left the town. Jack the Giant-Killer is so pleased with these good deeds that he becomes the prince's servant. They go to a giant's castle together. Jack tells the giant that a mighty prince is coming[1] and locks him up, so that the two take all his gold. Jack takes also an old coat and cap, a rusty sword, and a pair of slippers. They arrive at the lady's house. She tells the prince to show her in the morning a handkerchief, which she conceals in her dress. By putting on the coat of darkness, and the shoes of swiftness, and following her when she goes to

[1] See p. 62, note 2.

her demon lover, Jack gets the handkerchief for his master. Next day the lady tells the prince to get the lips which she will kiss the last that night. Jack follows her again and cuts off the demon's head, which the prince produces, thus breaking the spell that has bound her to the evil spirits.

This variant, even in what is probably a mutilated state, is strikingly similar to *Irish I.* in such details as the means used to follow the lady, and the tasks imposed upon the suitor. Indeed, the fact that the adventures take place in Wales might lead one to suppose that the story in this form was Celtic, were not the knowledge of it so persistent in England also. Several features are obscured, at least in the form from which I cite. Though the burial of the dead is given clearly enough, and the fact that the lady is possessed is insisted on, the prince is kind to an old woman as well as to a dead man, and Jack is certainly not understood to be a ghost. All mention of an agreement between the companions, and of the means taken to free the heroine from her possession by dividing her or flogging her, has likewise disappeared. However, the correspondence both in outline and in detail with *Irish I.* is sufficient to establish the position of the variant.

In the *Old Wives' Tale* the theme of *The Grateful Dead* is imbedded in such a mass of folk-lore and folk-tales that it is quite impossible to restore adequately the narrative as Peele found it. He treated the story as a literary artist, of course, modifying and adding details to suit the scheme of his play. The outline of the story, as Peele gives it, is as follows: A king, or a lord, or a duke, has a daughter as white as snow and as red as blood, who is carried off by a conjurer in the form of a dragon. Her two brothers set forth to seek her, and by a cross meet an old man named Erestus, who calls himself the White Bear of England's Wood.

He, they learn, has been enchanted by the conjurer, and is a man by day and a bear by night. He tells them of his own troubles, and gives them good advice. Later he is met by the wandering knight Eumenides, who likewise is seeking the lady Delia and is counselled:

> "Bestowe thy almes, give more than all,
> Till dead men's bones come at thy call."

Eumenides pays all his money except three farthings to bury the body of Jack, while the conjurer compels Delia to goad her brothers at the work to which he has set them. Eumenides is overtaken by the ghost of Jack, who becomes his servant, or "copartner," provides him with money, and slays the conjurer while invisible, thus breaking the spell of all the enchanted persons. Jack then demands his half of Delia, refuses to take her whole, and, when Eumenides prepares to cut her in twain, explains that he has asked this only as a trial of constancy. He quickly disappears.

Dutz has already shown[1] that *Old Wives' Tale* has three of the essential features of *The Grateful Dead*, viz.: the burial of the dead with the peculiar prophetic advice of Erestus, the reward of the hero by assistance in getting a wife, and the sharing of the woman. Because of the non-schematic nature of his discussion he did not make any attempt to classify the variant more specifically. In his edition of the play,[2] Professor Gummere, in indicating some of the folk-lore which Peele used, has likewise called attention[3] to the connection with our theme. Of particular importance is his hint as to the likeness of the variant to the story which I call *Irish III*. It is practicable, however, to carry the matter somewhat further. The adventures of Delia, Eumenides, and Jack are all that really concern us. It will be seen that

[1] Pp. 10 f.
[2] Gayley, *Representative English Comedies*, 1903, pp. 333-384.
[3] P. 345.

these conform in essentials to the type under consideration. There is the burial, the agreement, the death of
the wizard, and the division. To be sure, as in other
instances, the dispossession of the woman has been
obscured by other elements; yet the type is unmistakable, it seems to me. One trait in particular connects
Old Wives' Tale with *Irish I.* and *II.* In all three the
hero seeks a maiden who is white as snow and red as
blood. On the other hand, the ghost is called Jack as
in *Irish III.* and the English tale which bears Jack's
name. Because of these similarities and discrepancies
one is forced to conclude that for this part of his play
Peele drew upon some version of *Jack the Giant-Killer*,
which was far better preserved than the forms known
to-day. His original must have had many points in
common with the tale as extant in Ireland, though we
need not believe that he knew it in other than English
dress.

It yet remains to consider the relations of the two
sets of variants discussed in this chapter to *The Poison
Maiden* and to one another. The group is peculiar in
that all the members of it are folk-tales, save three:
Tobit, Danish III. and *Old Wives' Tale.* The two latter
are, however, immediately derived from popular narratives
of an easily discernible type. Thus *Tobit* is an anomaly
from almost any point of view, obscure in its origin and
possessed of only trivial influence upon the other tales
belonging to the same group. Of the twenty-six variants,
fifteen have *The Grateful Dead + The Poison Maiden*
simply, while the other eleven add thereto more or less
distinct elements of *The Water of Life.*

In the following versions the hero is saved on the
wedding night, or the bride is purified by some means:
*Tobit, Armenian, Gypsy, Siberian, Russian I., Russian II.,
Russian III., Russian IV., Russian V., Russian VI.,
Servian II., Servian III., Servian IV., Bulgarian,*

Esthonian II., Irish I., Irish II., Danish III., Norwegian II., and *Harz I.* Not all the stories which I have placed in the group, it will be observed, have this feature; but, out of all the variants of *The Grateful Dead* enumerated in the bibliographical list, not one has it except members of the group. Now this purification of the bride, by means of which the hero is saved, is precisely the element of *The Poison Maiden* which is most essential. There can be no doubt, therefore, that this theme actually united with a more primitive form of *The Grateful Dead* to form the compound discussed in this chapter. The combination must have been made very early and in Asia, as *Tobit* and *Armenian* bear witness. It will be noted that all the variants, save *Finnish*, which have the simple compound, retain the rescue of the bridegroom, while only half of those where a subsidiary motive has been introduced have the like. Apparently the intrusion of new matter of a very romantic sort tended to obscure the original climax of the combined type.

Another feature of much importance in this connection is the division of the woman, or whatever is substituted for it. In a large majority of the variants studied, which have the trait at all, the purpose of the division proposed or accomplished is to test the fidelity of the hero. Hippe believed [1] that this was a modification of the original trait, an opinion which would be justified if the compound type *The Grateful Dead + The Poison Maiden* only were considered. The versions which have the purification are the following: *Armenian, Gypsy, Siberian, Russian II., Russian IV., Russian V., Russian VI., Servian II., Servian III., Servian IV., Bulgarian, Esthonian II., Finnish, Irish I., Irish II.,* and *Old Wives' Tale.* In these the purpose of the division, or beating, whether actually performed or not, is the disposal of

[1] Pp. 176-178.

serpents or other venomous creatures by which the woman is possessed.[1] It will be noted, however, that all of these variants are of the type treated in the present chapter. If the division for the sake of purification were then regarded as more primitive and older than the division for the sake of sharing the gains or of testing the hero, it would naturally follow that all the combined types must proceed from *The Grateful Dead + The Poison Maiden.* Hippe followed the logical course from his premises in so regarding the relationship of the groups.[2] However, it seems clear to me—and it will be increasingly evident as we study the other groups— that the division for purification belongs solely to the compound treated in this chapter. It would follow logically from combining *The Poison Maiden,* where a friend saves the hero from the fatal embraces of a woman, with *The Grateful Dead,* where the hero is willing to divide his wife to satisfy the agreement which he has made with his benefactor. Only by such an explanation is it possible to account for the development of the several groups from a common root. The barbarous character of the division for purification, and the softening which it has undergone in the group which we have been studying, give it an appearance of antiquity to which it has no right. In point of fact, it belongs only to this group, which is thus clearly set off from all the others as an independent branch. The division for the sake of fulfilling an obligation is more widespread, though it has suffered many modifications.

[1] *Russian V.* and *VI.* are, of course, exceptions, since the woman is there a vampire.

[2] See his scheme on page 181.

CHAPTER V.

THE GRATEFUL DEAD AND *THE RANSOMED WOMAN*.

As has already been shown,[1] Simrock regarded as an essential feature of *The Grateful Dead* the release of a maiden from captivity by the hero. Stephens and Hippe [2] saw that such was not the case. The latter's treatment of the matter [3] leaves little to be desired as far as it goes, save that it implies a derivation of the compound *The Grateful Dead + The Ransomed Woman* from the compound treated in the last chapter—a view which I believe erroneous.

The Ransomed Woman appears as a separate tale or in combination with other themes than *The Grateful Dead* more than once. A prolonged study of the motive would probably yield a rich harvest of examples, though it is sufficient for the present purpose to refer to Hippe's article as establishing the existence of the form. His Wendish folk-tale [4] and *Guter Gerhard*, from the latter of which Simrock started his enquiry, are of themselves evidence enough.[5] Neither example has anything whatever to do with *The Grateful Dead*.[6] The characteristics

---

[1] See above, p. 1.   [2] See above, pp. 2 and 5.

[3] Pp. 170-175.   [4] P. 173.

[5] See also the school drama cited by Köhler, *Germania III.* 208 f. The elements of *Der gute Gerhard*, foreign to *The Ransomed Woman*, I have treated in the *Publications of the Modern Lang. Ass.* 1905, xx. 529-545.

[6] The same is true of the story related of St. Catharine, analyzed by Simrock, pp. 110-113, and cited by Hippe, p. 166, from *Scala Celi*, by

of *The Ransomed Woman* will appear as we consider the compound type, which contains folk-tales almost exclusively, as was the case with the type studied in the previous chapter, but in most cases from Western Europe instead of from both Asia and Europe.

Nineteen variants have *The Grateful Dead* and *The Ransomed Woman* combined in a comparatively simple form without admixture with related themes. These are : *Servian I., Lithuanian I.,*[1] *Hungarian II., Transylvanian, Catalan, Spanish, Trancoso, Nicholas, Gasconian, Straparola I., Istrian, Gaelic, Breton III.,*[2] *Swedish, Norwegian I., Icelandic I.* and *II.,* and *Simrock IV.* and *VI.*

In *Servian I.* a merchant's son, while on a journey, ransoms a company of slaves whom he finds in the hands of freebooters. Among them is a beautiful maiden with her nurse. He marries the lady, who proves to be the daughter of an emperor. On a second voyage he ransoms two peasants, who have been imprisoned for not paying their taxes to the emperor. On his third journey he comes to his father-in-law's court, and is sent back for his wife. He is, however, cast into the sea by a former lover of the princess, and succeeds in getting ashore on a lonely island, where he remains for fifteen days and fifteen nights.[3] Then an angel in the disguise of an old man appears to him, and, on condition of receiving half of his possessions, brings him to court, where he is

Johannes Junior (Gobius), under *Castitas.* Hippe, as shown by his scheme on p. 181, places this under "Legendarische Formen mit Loskauf." As a matter of fact, it is plainly a specimen of *The Calumniated Woman.*

[1] Hippe's "Lithuanian II."

[2] *Breton III.*, though placed here, has peculiar traits, which require special consideration.

[3] Köhler, followed by Hippe, p. 145, makes the hero live for fifteen years on the island, while Mme. Mijatovich gives the time as stated. As I have no knowledge of Servian, I cannot tell which is in the right. Hippe's analysis is otherwise faulty.

reunited with his wife. After renouncing his claim, the old man explains who he is, and disappears.

The most striking peculiarity of the variant is the loss of the burial, for which appears rather awkwardly the ransoming of some peasants on the hero's second voyage. That substitution has occurred is apparent, however, both from the clumsiness of the device by which the original trait is replaced, and from the angel in the form of an old man, who takes the rôle of the ghost. It will be remembered that the same substitution has already been met with in the case of *Tobit* and *Russian II.*

In *Lithuanian I.* is found a variant which, as we shall find, is of a common type. A king's son pays three hundred gold-pieces, all that he possesses, to release a dead man from his creditors and have him buried. The hero then becomes a merchant, and finds a princess on an island, whither she has been driven by a storm. He takes her to a city, where he makes his home, and marries her. A messenger, sent out by her father to seek her, arrives, takes them aboard ship, and pitches the hero into the sea in order to obtain the offered reward. He is saved by a man in a boat, who says that he is the ghost of the dead, and instructs him how to rejoin his bride. So everything ends happily.

The events as here related follow a very normal course, which is repeated again and again in stories of this type : a burial, a ransom, an act of treachery, a rescue by the ghost, and a happy reunion of the lovers. The agreement between the hero and the ghost, which is found in *Servian I.*, and very frequently elsewhere, is lacking, however. A peculiarity of the variant is the change in status of the hero. He is a prince, but becomes a merchant, thus uniting the two characters given him in the other tales of this class.

Hungarian II. is in some respects more interesting than the variant just cited. A merchant's son while in

Turkey pays the debts and for the burial of a mistreated corpse. After returning home, he goes to England and rescues a French princess with her two maids, but by his cunning saves the gold that he has agreed to pay for them. At her bidding he goes to Paris and tells the king that she is safe. On his return to bring her to her home, where he is to marry her, he is placed on a desert island by a general who is enamoured of the princess. Thence he is rescued by an old man, the ghost of the dead, who takes him to the Continent. He goes to Paris, where he is recognised by the princess, when he drops a ring that she has given him into a beaker. When she comes to him in his room, he threatens to kill her if she does not go away; but when she agrees that he has the right to do so since he has saved her life, he says that his threat was only a test of loyalty. So the story ends happily.

The course of events is not very different from that of *Lithuanian I.*, since the variant has all the normal elements save the agreement between the ghost and the hero. A peculiarity is the final scene in which the hero tests his lady. It will be evident, I think, that this is an obscured and modified form of the test to which the ghost elsewhere submits the hero, a test of fidelity likewise, though different in its nature.

In the *Transylvanian* variant, a merchant's son while on a journey pays fifty florins, half of his capital, for the burial of a dead man. On a second journey he pays one hundred florins, again one-half of his store, for the ransom of a princess who has been imprisoned while out doing charity *incognito*. She gives him a ring and sends him to the castle, where her father turns him out of doors. He then meets an old man—the ghost—and promises him one-half of his gains after seven years for his help. He is then enabled to marry the princess, who recognizes him at the castle by his ring. They have two children. When the old man comes back at the end of seven years, the hero gives up one of his children, and, after offering her whole, is ready to divide his wife. The old man renounces his claim, and disappears.

Every step in the narrative is here clearly marked, even to the conditional agreement with the ghost, which so frequently is wanting. The variant thus appears to be entirely normal as far as *The Grateful Dead* goes, though it does not have the rescue by the ghost—an important feature of *The Ransomed Woman.*

In *Catalan*[1] a young man on a journey has a poor man buried at his expense, and ransoms a princess. Later he goes to the court of her parents with a flag on which she has embroidered her name. They recognise this, and send the youth back for the lady. On the way he is cast into the sea by the sailors, but is saved by the thankful dead and brought to the court again, where he espouses the princess.

In *Spanish*[2] a young Venetian merchant pays the debts of a Christian at Tunis, and has him buried. At the house of the creditor he also buys a Christian slave girl. He takes her back to Venice and marries her. At the wedding a sea-captain recognizes the lady, and lures the couple aboard his ship. The young man is cast into the sea, but by clinging to a plank reaches land, where he lives seven months with a hermit. At the end of that time he is sent to the coast, where he finds a ship, and is transported to Ireland. There he is entrusted by the captain with two letters to the king. The one says that he is a great physician, who will heal the sick princess; the other that the plank, the hermit, and the captain who has brought him to Ireland are one and all the ghost of the man whom he buried. The hero is recognized at court by the princess, who has

[1] See Hippe, p. 151. [2] *Ibid.*

been brought thither by the traitor, and has explained all to her father.

In these tales the theme of *The Grateful Dead* is somewhat abbreviated for the sake of the romantic features of the secondary motive. In both, the agreement with the ghost and every trace of a division have disappeared, though they differ in the details of the treachery by which the lovers are separated. In the former[1] much is made of the manner by which the hero gets a favourable reception at the court of the princess's father, while in the latter this is suppressed. Recognition by some such means, it will appear, is an important feature of the majority of the variants in this section. It must be remembered, of course, that *Spanish* is a semi-literary version, even though popular in origin.

Trancoso, the work of a sixteenth century Portuguese story-teller, is even more consciously literary. It shows, besides, the tendency of the narrative to take on a religious colouring. The son of a Lusitanian merchant, while in Fez on a trading expedition, buys the relics of a Christian saint. In spite of his father's anger, he does this a second time, and is so successful in retailing the bones that he is sent out a third time with instructions to buy as many relics as possible. On this expedition, however, he succeeds merely in ransoming a Christian girl, whom he takes home. At her request he carries to the King of England a piece of linen, on which she has embroidered the story of her adventures. He learns that she is the king's daughter, and restores her to her father. Subsequently he wanders over Europe in despair, for he has hoped to marry the princess, till he meets with two minstrels, who accompany him to the English court. There he makes himself known to the princess

---

[1] Hippe fails to note that the hero used all his money on the first journey in burying the dead, and that it was on a second trip that he bought the king's daughter.

F

by a song; and, by the aid of the two minstrels, he wins her hand in a tournament. Later the two friends reveal themselves as the saints whose bones he had rescued from the Moors.

Though this version clearly belongs in the category now under discussion, it has certain features that can be explained only on the supposition that Trancoso altered his source to suit his personal fancy. The clever substitute for actual burial, the duplication of that trait (which occurs nowhere else), the humorous touch with reference to the hero's success in selling relics, and the appearance of the ghosts as minstrels, are all strokes of individual invention. The wanderings of the hero and his manner of revealing himself to the princess are doubtless reminiscences from the popular romances of Spain, while the tournament probably comes, as Menéndez y Pelayo hints,[1] from an earlier version of our theme, *Oliver*, which will be treated below. In spite of these peculiarities, the ordinary features of the combined theme are not more obscured than in the two preceding variants. The agreement, the division, and the rescue are the only ones that disappear.

In the fourteenth century variant from *Scala Celi*, *Nicholas*, our story is altogether transformed into a legend. The only son of a widow[2] of Bordeaux is sent as a merchant to a distant city with fifty pounds. He gives it all to help rebuild a church of St. Nicholas, and returns home empty-handed. Much later he is sent out with one hundred pounds, and buys the Sultan's daughter. His mother disowns him, and he is supported by the embroidery which the princess makes. With her wares he goes to a festival at Alexandria, but, at her bidding, keeps away from the castle. When he journeys to

[1] *Orígenes de la Novela*, ii. xcv.

[2] An odd inconsistency appears in the statement of the Latin that after the hero's second voyage " pater suus et mater " were angry with him.

Alexandria a second time, however, he goes to the castle and is imprisoned, as the handiwork of the princess is recognized. She is sent for, while the hero is released and goes home. Since he does not find the maiden there, he returns to Alexandria with a piece of embroidery which she has sent him, meets her, and elopes by the aid of St. Nicholas, who sends them a ship opportunely.

Because of its legendary character the variant has been materially transformed, but not beyond recognition. The thankful dead is replaced by the saint throughout, so that the burial is altered into church building, and both the agreement and the division of the gains disappear. The various elements of *The Ransomed Woman* fare better: the act of treachery done the hero is the only one lacking, and that perhaps is replaced by his imprisonment in the Sultan's castle. It is remarkable that the details of the narrative have been so little altered in spite of its complete change of purpose.

In the *Gasconian* folk-tale Jean du Boucau, the son of a mariner, goes to fight the corsairs. On the shore of the sea he rescues a man named Uartia, who is pretending death to escape from his creditors. Later this man becomes a prosperous freebooter, and is sailing with a load of captives when met again by Jean. The latter is so shocked by his evil deeds that he encloses him in the coffin prepared for him on the previous occasion, and throws him into the sea. Jean then marries the most beautiful of the captives, who is the daughter of the King of Bilbao.

The variant is excessively rationalized, it will be observed, and most traces of *The Grateful Dead* have disappeared. Though various substitutions for the burial are found in each of the groups, this is the only case that I know where the man plays 'possum to escape his creditors. The story is likewise unique in making the hero take vengeance on the man whom he has helped earlier, and accordingly in making him rescue the maiden from the hands of the person who is in the character of the thankful dead. The variant has been modified by a free fancy; yet its position in the group remains perfectly clear in spite of the loss of such traits as the agreement, the act of treachery, the rescue of the hero, and the division of the gains.

Straparola I., one of the Italian novelist's two renderings of our theme, is far more normal than the above, and is probably based directly on a folk-story. Bertuccio pays one hundred ducats to free a corpse from a robber and bury it, greatly to his mother's disgust. He goes out again with two hundred ducats, and pays them for the ransom of the daughter of the King of Navarre. His mother is still more angry. The princess is taken home to Navarre by officers of the court who have been searching for her, but first she tells Bertuccio to come to her, and to hold his hand to his head as a sign when he hears that she is to be married. On his way to Navarre he meets a knight who gives him a horse and clothing on condition of his returning them, together with half of his gains. He marries the princess, and is returning home, when he meets the knight again and offers to give up his wife whole rather than kill her by division. Whereupon the knight explains that he is the spirit of the dead, and resigns his claim.

All the traits previously mentioned are here evident save the act of treachery by which the hero comes near losing his bride. The sign appears as a means of communication between the lovers, as in *Transylvanian* and elsewhere. The question of division is simply a matter of fulfilling a bargain, but it shows how easily by a slight shift of emphasis the test of loyalty could be made the important element.

None of the Italian folk variants, which I know, conforms to the above closely enough to be regarded as a near relative. *Istrian*, however, belongs in the same category. A youth called Fair Brow sets out to trade with six thousand *scudi*, which he pays to bury a debtor on the shore, for whom passers-by are giving alms. On his return home, he tells his father that he has been robbed, and again is sent out with six thousand *scudi*. He pays these for a maiden, who has been stolen from the Sultan, and he is consequently disowned by his father. After his marriage to the girl, the young couple live by the sale of the wife's paintings. Some sailors of the Sultan see these, and carry the lady off home. Fair Brow goes fishing with an old man whom he meets by the sea. They are driven by a storm to Turkey, and are sold to the Sultan as slaves, but they escape with the wife and considerable treasure. The old man then asks for a division of the property, even of the woman. When the hero offers him three-quarters of the wealth in order to keep the woman, the old man declares that he is the ghost, and disappears.

All of the essential traits, except the preliminary agreement and the rescue of the hero, are here clearly marked. The latter is, indeed, probably accounted for by the storm which the hero and the ghost encounter together. The fact that the young couple live by the sale of the wife's handiwork, and that this in some way or other leads to her restoration to her parents or earlier connections, is an important feature of *The Ransomed Woman*, being found clearly in the Wendish tale as well as in many variants of the compound type.

Gaelic is an interesting example of the theme. Iain, the son of a Barra widow, becomes the master of a ship and goes to Turkey, where he pays the debts of a dead Christian and buries the corpse. He ransoms a Christian maiden, the daughter of the King of Spain, with her servant, on the same journey, and takes her back to England, together with much gold. At her advice he goes to Spain and attends church, where the king recog-. nizes by his clothing, his ring, his book, and his whistle that he has news of the lost princess. Iain then returns to England for the maiden, whom he is to marry. While going with her to Spain he is left on a desert island by a general, who has secreted himself on the ship; but after a time he is rescued by a man in a boat, to whom he promises half of his wife and of his children, if he shall have any. In Spain the princess, who has gone mad, recognizes him when he plays his whistle. So they are married, and the general burned. When three sons have been born, the rescuer appears and asks for his share; but as soon as Iain accedes he declares himself to be the ghost, and disappears.

Apart from the dressing of the story, which is unusually good, the variant follows the normal course. The several signs by which the hero is recognized by the king and the princess mark the imaginative wealth of the Celt, though the appearance of a ring, and the fact that the hero is left on a desert island by an infatuated general, show a close correspondence with *Hungarian II.* The introduction of the children as part of the property to be divided is interesting, since it shows the connecting link by which the simple compound now under consideration passed into combination with the theme of *The Two Friends.*[1] *Gaelic,* however, clearly belongs where it is here placed. The healing of the princess at the hero's coming reminds one of the similar trait in *Spanish.*

Breton III.[2] is peculiar in several ways. A young man, who had been unjustly cast off by his parents, put himself under the protection of St. Corentin and the Virgin. To an old woman he gave all his stock of money that she might bury her husband and have

---

[1] So, too, with *Transylvanian.* See above, pp. 79 f.

[2] See Hippe, p. 150.

masses said for his soul. The saint and the Virgin then led the hero to a nobleman, whose daughter he married. On a hunt he was cast into the sea by an envious uncle of his wife, at a time when she was pregnant; but he was brought to an island by some mysterious power and nourished there for five years by St. Corentin. Finally an old man appeared and took him home after he had promised half of his possessions to the rescuer. When a year had passed, the old man came back and demanded half of the child; but just as the mysterious stranger was about to divide the child St. Corentin and the Virgin appeared and explained their identity, together with that of the old man, who was the saint himself. They told the hero, furthermore, that God was well pleased with him, and would take his son and himself to Paradise. Father and son fell dead immediately, while the wife went into a convent.

This tale, like *Nicholas,* has been dressed up as a legend, chiefly in the praise of St. Corentin, with the result that the elements are confused. The burial, however, persists, though the ransoming of the woman has been feebly replaced by the aid of the saint and the Virgin. The hero is cast into the sea by an avaricious uncle of the bride, again a weakened trait. The rescue and the agreement to divide are normal in essentials, though adorned with superfluous miracles, as is again the conclusion of the tale. It illustrates how easily such a narrative may be adapted, whether consciously or not, to a religious purpose. The division of the child, which comes in question, is of precisely the same character as in *Gaelic;* it does not imply the presence of a new motive, though it indicates the possibility of a new combination.

Swedish[1] is a somewhat abbreviated form of the normal type. Pelle Båtsman, while on a journey, pays

---

[1] See Hippe, p. 158.

the debts of a dead man, and so brings repose to him; for he has been hunted from his grave and soundly beaten every night by his creditors, who are likewise dead. Pelle then falls in with robbers, with whom he finds the daughter of the King of Armenia. He escapes with her, and goes on board a ship to seek her father, but he is thrown overboard by the envious captain. He is saved by the thankful dead and brought to Armenia, where he marries the princess. Here the burial is peculiar in that the dead man is harassed by creditors who are already dead. This is a marvel, which need excite no surprise in view of the modifications of the trait found elsewhere. The ransom in this case does not imply a money payment, since the hero escapes from robbers with the maiden. The way in which the hero is left behind by the master of the vessel on which the lovers sail is a trait similar to the one in *Catalan* and *Spanish*. The agreement between the hero and the ghost, the sign employed by the hero, and the division of gains are all lacking; but no new feature replaces them.

Norwegian I.[1] is not very different from the preceding tale. A man in the service of a merchant pays all he has, while on one voyage, to bury the body of a dead man. On his next voyage he ransoms a princess, and sets out with her for England. On the way she is carried off by her brother and a former suitor. The hero overtakes them and is given a ring by the lady, but is cast into the sea by the suitor. For seven years he lives on a desert isle, till an old man appears, tells him that it is the princess's bridal day, carries him to England, and gives him a flask. This the hero sends to his lady, is thus recognized, and is married. The agreement with the ghost and the division of the woman are entirely lacking, though the burial, the ransom, the treachery of the suitor, and the aid of

---

[1] Hippe's brief analysis, p. 159, fails to give a satisfactory outline.

the ghost apppear in normal fashion. The sign enters only as a means of communication between the lovers. The tale thus has no very unusual traits.

Icelandic I.[1] is a fuller, and, for our purpose, more interesting variant than the last. Thorsteinn, a king's son, who has wasted his substance, sells his kingdom and sets forth into the world. He pays two hundred rix-dollars to free from debt a dead man, whose grave is beaten every day by a creditor to destroy his rest. The prince goes on, and in the castle of a giant finds a princess hanging by the hair. He frees her, and is taking her home when he meets Raudr, a knight to whom her hand has been promised if he can find her. Raudr puts the prince to sea alone in a boat and carries the lady home. Thorsteinn, however, is brought thither also by the ghost and is recognized by the princess, when she is about to be married to the traitor. So Raudr is punished, and Thorsteinn obtains the princess.

Here, again, the agreement, the sign, and the division do not appear, though the version is otherwise normal. To be sure, the ransom of the lady is replaced by a rescue, as in *Swedish*, and the beating of the grave preserves a bit of northern superstition, which is interesting even though not primitive as far as our tale is concerned.[2]

Icelandic II. is similar to the variant just cited in several particulars, though it has important differences. Vilhjálmur, a merchant's son, loses his property and becomes the servant of twelve robbers. In their den he finds a princess named Ása hanging by the hair. He escapes with her by sea, taking along the thieves' treasure. This he pays to have the body of a debtor buried. To

---

[1] Hippe's analysis, p. 159, is not quite adequate.

[2] *Russian I.* is the only other variant that I know which makes the dead man uneasy in his grave.

the haven where this happens comes Rauður in search of the princess, takes the couple on his ship, but puts the hero to sea in a rudderless boat. A man appears to Vilhjálmur in a dream, saying that he is the ghost of the man whom he has buried, and that he will bring him to land and show him treasure. So the hero is brought to the land of the princess and tells his story at the wedding of the traitor with the princess. Thus the bride is won for him.

The hero, it will be observed, is a merchant instead of a prince, as in *Icelandic I.*, and the burial of the dead is customary in form though exceptionally placed in the narrative. Otherwise the two variants correspond rather closely, even in such a detail as the name of the traitor. There is the same omission of elements peculiar to *The Grateful Dead*, the same preponderance of the secondary motive, found in all the northern versions of this particular group. The two Icelandic variants seem to be perfectly distinct, though they are nearly related.

The two German folk-tales which fall into this group are not very different from one another. In *Simrock IV.* a merchant's son pays the debts of a man who is being devoured by dogs, but does not succeed in saving his life. He goes on, finds two maidens exposed on a rock, and takes them home. In spite of his father's objections, he marries one of them. He goes to sea again, wearing a ring that his wife has given him, and carrying a flag marked with her name. Coming to the royal court of her father, he is sent back for the princess with a minister. On his voyage to court again he is put overboard by the minister, who hopes thus to win the princess. However, he is cast up on an island, where the ghost of the dead man appears to him in sleep and transports him miraculously to court. There he is recognized by his ring and reunited to his wife.

Details such as those concerning the burial, the rescue

of the lady, and the help given miraculously by the ghost mark the independence of the variant, though they do not alter the normal course of the narrative. As so often in this group, the agreement with the ghost and the division are entirely lacking.

In *Simrock VI.* the variations from the normal are even slighter. Heinrich of Hamburg buys a beautiful maiden in a foreign land. On the sea-coast, when he is returning home with her, he pays the debts of a corpse and has it buried. He wishes to marry the girl, but she asks that he delay the wedding for a year and make a journey first. So she gives him two coffers, with which he crosses the sea. By the help of a shipman he finds his betrothed's royal father, but on his way back to fetch her home is cast overboard by the mariner, who is the original kidnapper of the maiden. This man gets her and carries her to the court with the hope of marrying her. The hero is saved from the sea, however, by the ghost of the dead man, who brings him to the garden of the princess's palace, where he is found by his bride.

The order of the burial and the ransoming[1] is here reversed, but the facts are given in the ordinary form. Otherwise the variant does not differ essentially from the preceding.

In *Transylvanian,*[2] and more clearly in *Gaelic* and *Breton III.,*[3] a tendency has been remarked to introduce the children of the hero as part of the gains which he is asked to divide with the thankful ghost. In a series of tales belonging to the general type *The Grateful Dead + The Ransomed Woman* this tendency has been accentuated so far that it seems best to group them together, because of their approach to the theme of *The Two Friends.* Since an actual combination of this motive

---

[1] So also in *Servian I.* and *Icelandic II.*, cited above, as well as *Bohemian* and *Simrock VII.*, for which see below.

[2] See pp. 79 f.   [3] See pp. 85-87.

with *The Grateful Dead* in its simple form is found in only three variants, all of them literary, it will perhaps be best to discuss the relationship of the main to the minor theme at this point.

The Two Friends is the chief motive of *Amis and Amiloun*, which in its various forms[1] is the mediaeval epic of ideal friendship. Its essential feature, as far as the present study is concerned, is the sacrifice of his two sons by Amis to cure the leprosy of Amiloun. They are actually slain, but are miraculously brought to life again by the power of God. This story, which exercised a powerful influence on the imagination of European peoples, easily became connected with the sacrifice of his wife by the hero of *The Grateful Dead.*

The three variants with the simple compound, or forming a group on that basis, are those entered in the bibliography as *Lope de Vega, Calderon,* and *Oliver.*

The plot of *Oliver* runs as follows[2]: Oliver, the son of the King of Castille, becomes the close friend of Arthur of Algarbe, the son of his stepmother. When he has grown up, he flees from home because of the love which the queen declares for him, leaving to Arthur a vial in which the water would grow dark, were he to come into danger. He is shipwrecked while on his way to Constantinople, but, together with another knight, is saved miraculously by a stag, which carries them to England. Talbot, the other knight, is ill, and asks Oliver to take him to his home at Canterbury, where he dies. Because of debts that his parents will not pay he cannot be buried in consecrated ground till Oliver him-

---

[1] See *Amis et Amiles und Jourdains de Blaivies*, ed. K. Hofmann, 2nd ed. 1882; *Amis und Amiloun zugleich mit der altfranzösischen Quelle*, ed. E. Kölbing, 1884, with the comprehensive discussion of versions in the introduction; also Kölbing, "Zur Ueberlieferung der Sage von Amicus und Amelius," in Paul und Braune's *Beiträge* iv. 271-314; etc.

[2] Hippe's analysis, p. 156, is different from mine, and is taken from a less trustworthy source. I use the summary of the Ghent text.

self attends to the matter. The hero then starts for a tourney where the hand of the king's daughter is the prize. On the way he loses his horse and money, but is supplied anew by a mysterious knight, on condition of receiving half of what he gets at the tourney. Here he is victor, and after a further successful war in Ireland marries the princess, who bears him two children. While hunting he is taken prisoner by the King of Ireland and placed in a dungeon. Arthur, who is acting as regent in Spain, notices that the vial has grown dark, and sets out to rescue his brother. In Ireland he is wounded by a dragon, but is healed by a white knight, who notices his resemblance to Oliver, and takes him to London to solace the princess. He only escapes her embraces by the pretence of a vow, and sets forth to deliver Oliver. On their way back he tells of his visit at London, and so excites Oliver's jealousy, who leaves him. At home, however, Oliver discovers his mistake, and determines to find his brother, who, after a punitive expedition into Ireland, falls gravely ill. Oliver learns in a dream that Arthur can only be cured by the blood of his children, whom he slays accordingly. On his return home, however, he finds them as well as ever. Later appears the mysterious knight to demand his share of wife and children, as well as of all his property. As Oliver raises his sword to divide his wife, he is told to desist, since his loyalty is proved. The knight then explains that he is the ghost of Talbot. Later Arthur marries Oliver's daughter, and eventually unites the kingdoms of England, Castille, and Algarbe.

Oliver has certain elements not to be accounted for by the combination of *The Two Friends* with *The Grateful Dead*. Such are the motive of the hero's journey, for example, which allies it with the tales of incestuous step-mothers; and the tourney in which the hero wins his bride. Yet the burial of the dead man (here a knight and a friend of the hero's)[1] corresponds to the normal form of the episode in that Oliver pays the creditors and the sum necessary for the man's interment. So, too, the demand made by the ghost for half of all that has been won runs true to the original form. The distinctive trait of *Amis and Amiloun*, at the same time, comes out more clearly than in the case of such folk-tales as *Gaelic*—the hero actually kills his little children to save the life of his old friend and foster-brother. One factor leads me to think that the romance and the two romantic plays are to be regarded as forms of the general type treated in this chapter, with additions from other stories. The ghost rescues the hero from imprisonment. A rescue of the sort—normally after the hero has been cast into the sea or left behind by his rival— is characteristic of *The Grateful Dead + The Ransomed Woman*. In *Oliver* this rescue takes place, to be sure, after the marriage instead of before, which is the normal order, yet it is a factor of considerable importance. The romance takes a position somewhat apart; and even though this is partly due to the literary handling which it has undergone, it must remain doubtfully classed with the immediate circle of variants belonging to the compound type.

The position of the play by *Lope de Vega* is involved with that of *Oliver*. Don Juan de Castro flees to England because of the unlawful love of his stepmother, the Princess of Galicia. His ship is wrecked on the English coast, and the captain, Tibaldo, is cast ashore in a dying condition. To free the latter's mind from unrest, Don Juan pays his debts of two thousand ducats, though this is half of the hero's possessions. He hears that the princess Clarinda is promised to anyone of princely blood who wins an approaching tournament. While he

[1] See p. 49 for other tales in which the dead man is a friend of the hero's.

is sorrowful that he cannot enter the contest, because of his poverty, the ghost of Tibaldo appears to him one night and promises the necessary equipment on condition of receiving one-half the gains. The next morning he finds everything ready and wins the princess. He is later taken prisoner by one of the contestants through a ruse, and is carried off to Ireland. By the ghost's advice, his stepbrother and double comes to London and takes his place, while Don Juan is freed by force of arms and restored to his wife. After some years, when the couple have two children, the stepbrother falls ill of a dreadful malady, which can only be cured, Don Juan learns in a dream, by the blood of his children. So he slays them and gives their blood to the sick man to drink. They are found alive by a miracle; but Don Juan is troubled, and does not find rest till the ghost appears and tells him that the only remedy for his affliction is to fulfil his promise of a division. The hero prepares to divide his wife, when the ghost stops him and explains that the demand was only a test.

As Schaeffer pointed out,[1] Lope's plot is clearly taken from *Oliver*, probably from the Spanish translation issued in 1499. Indeed, the drama follows the romance with far more fidelity than could have been expected of such an adaptation. The various elements of the motive appear without essential alteration.

The play *El mejor amigo el muerto*, listed for convenience as *Calderon*, has suffered, in contrast to Lope's play, from many changes. Prince Robert of Ireland and Don Juan de Castro are wrecked on the English coast. The former finds the sea-captain Lidoro in a dying condition, and refuses to give him aid. Don Juan, on the other hand, finds Lidoro's body, which a creditor keeps from interment, and pays for his burial out of his scanty savings from the wreck. He then goes to London,

[1] *Geschichte des spanischen Nationaldramas*, i. 141.

where there is trouble because Queen Clarinda will not marry Prince Robert. Don Juan is cast into prison on a false charge, his identity being unknown to the queen, though he is recognized by Robert. He is saved by the aid of Lidoro's ghost, nevertheless, lays siege for Clarinda's hand, overcomes Robert, and so becomes king of England.

The correspondence of names and details makes it clear that the source of this play is *Lope de Vega*, though the plot has been modified in several features. In the process of adaptation all trace of *The Two Friends* has dropped out, a fact which would make the position of the variant difficult to ascertain, had the authors not left most of the characters their original names. The change in the position of the rescue of the hero from prison, indeed, gives a specious resemblance to the normal type *The Grateful Dead + The Ransomed Woman*, which is quite unjustified by the real state of the case.

All the other variants in which there is question of dividing a child, save one,[1] are folk-tales; and all of them save three[2] clearly belong in the category now under discussion. If they did not group themselves in this way, I should be unwilling even to consider the possibility of any general influence from *The Two Friends* upon these tales, since the only trait borrowed by any of them is precisely the division. Only in *Oliver* and *Lope de Vega* is this sacrifice made for the healing of a friend; and we have seen in the case of *Transylvanian*, *Gaelic*, and *Breton III.* how naturally the division of the child grows out of the division of the wife. As the matter stands, however, the case for the influence of *The Two Friends* is sufficiently strong to warrant the grouping of these tales together. The general

---

[1] *Sir Amadas*, for which see p. 37.

[2] *Irish I.*, for which see pp. 62 and 64, *Breton I.*, p. 65, and *Sir Amadas.*

relationship of the theme may be deferred to a later chapter.[1]

Lithuanian II.[2] is a characteristic specimen of the class of tales just referred to. A prince, while travelling, sees a corpse gnawed by swine in a street. He pays the man's creditors for his release and has the body buried. Later, on the same journey, he buys two maidens, one of whom is a king's daughter, and takes them home. After a year he goes on a second journey with the princess's picture for a figure-head on his ship, and a ring, which she has given him. The picture is recognized by the maiden's father, and the prince is sent back in the company of certain nobles to fetch her. While they are returning to her home with the princess, one of the nobles pushes the prince overboard. He lives on an island for two years, until a man comes to him and promises to bring him to court before the princess marries the traitor, on condition of receiving his first-born son. The agreement is made, and the prince wins his bride. After a son has been born to them, the man appears and demands the child. He is put off for fifteen years, and at the end of that time explains that he is the ghost of the rescued dead man.

All the traits of the compound type, as it has already been analyzed, are here apparent, save that the sacrifice of the child is substituted for that of the wife. The variant does not demand any further comment.

We come now to the various forms of *Jean de Calais*, which make up a little group by themselves. The ten examples of the story that I have been able to find differ from one another sufficiently to make separate analyses of most of them necessary.

The version by Mme. de Gomez (*I.*) runs as follows :[3] Jean, the son of a rich merchant at Calais, while on a journey, comes to the city of Palmanie on the island of

[1] vii.   [2] Hippe's *Lithauische III.*   [3] See Hippe, pp. 156 f.

G

Orimanie. There he pays the debts and secures the burial of a corpse which is being devoured by dogs. He also ransoms two slave girls, one of whom he marries and takes home. The woman is the daughter of the King of Portugal. While taking her to her father's court, Jean is separated from her by a treacherous general, but is saved by the grateful dead, and enabled to rejoin his wife. Later the ghost, who appears in the form of a man, demands half of their son according to the agreement of division which they have made. When Jean gives him the child to divide, the stranger praises his loyalty and disappears.

This story has all the characteristics of the type *The Grateful Dead* + *The Ransomed Woman* + the demand that the hero's son be divided. In general outline it is scarcely distinguishable from *Lithuanian II.*, save that the hero Jean is a merchant's son instead of a prince. In details, however, it differs considerably. For example, Jean marries one of the captive maidens as soon as he buys her; there is no question of signs by which the hero is recognized by his wife's father or by the princess herself; and the ghost is less dilatory in his demands. Some of these differences are doubtless to be accounted for through the unfaithfulness of the rendering, which is semi-literary.

At all events, *Jean de Calais III., IV.*, and *V.*, all three of which were heard on the Riviera, have several changes from *I.*, though they vary from one another only in very minor matters.[1] A single analysis will suffice for the three. Jean de Calais, the son of a merchant, on his first voyage gives all his profits to bury the corpse of a deceased debtor. On his second he ransoms a beautiful woman (with or without a com-

---

[1] Thus *III.* makes the princess a daughter of the King of Portugal, as in *I.* ; *IV.* gives no names whatever ; and *V.* makes the heroine's father King of England.

panion), and lives with her in poverty because of his father's displeasure. On a subsequent voyage he bears her portrait on the prow of the ship, where it is seen by her father. A former suitor meets him on his return to court with his wife (in *III.* goes with him) and throws him into the sea either by violence or by a ruse. He is cast up on an island (in *III.* is carried thither in a boat by the ghost in human form), whence he is conveyed by the ghost, on condition of receiving half of his first son, or half of what he loves best, to the court just as the princess is to marry the traitor. By a ruse he enters the palace and is recognized. Later the ghost appears, but stays Jean when he is about to sacrifice his son.

Jean de Calais VI., though from Brittany instead of southern France, does not differ greatly from the above, nor from *I.* Jean buries the dead man and ransoms two women on a single voyage, as in *I.* He is kindly received at home in spite of his extravagance, in which the variant differs from *III.*, *IV.*, and *V.*, and he marries one of the maidens there. On his next voyage the King of Portugal (as in *I.* and *III.*) recognizes his daughter's portrait and that of her maid, which the hero has displayed on his ship. He brings his wife to the court, after which they go back, together with a former suitor, for their possessions. On the voyage Jean is thrown overboard, but is washed up on an island, whither the ghost comes, announces himself immediately, and bargains rescue for half of the hero's child. Jean is transported to court miraculously, and there meets with the customary adventures at the close of the tale.

The variant is chiefly peculiar, it will be remarked, in placing the treachery of the former suitor after the marriage has been recognized by the king, and in making the ghost announce himself at once. Jean makes no blind bargain, a fact which detracts somewhat from the interest.

Jean de Calais II. and *VII.* differ from the other forms of the story in several ways. In the former[1] Jean is the son of a rich merchant, and has wasted much money. He is sent out to seek his fortune on land with seven thousand pistoles, but he pays his all for the debts and burial of a poor man. On his return, he is commended by his father, but again falls into evil ways. Once more he is sent forth with seven thousand pistoles, and passes the cemetery where he buried the debtor. As he does so, a great white bird speaks from the cross, saying that it is the soul of the dead man and will not forget. Jean buys the two daughters of the King of Portugal from a pirate and takes them home, where, with his complaisant father's approval, he marries the elder. Later he journeys to Lisbon with the portraits of the sisters, which are recognized by the king.[2] He is sent back for his wife, but is pushed overboard by a traitor, being driven on a rock in the sea, where he is fed by the white bird. Meanwhile, the traitor goes to Calais and remains there seven years as a suitor for the princess's hand. He is about to be rewarded, when Jean, after promising half of what he loves best to the white bird, is miraculously transported to Calais, whither the King of Portugal comes at the same time. The white bird bears witness to the hero's identity, and demands half of his child. When Jean is about to divide the boy, however, it stops him and flies away.

Version *VII.* has certain characteristics in common with the above. It is a Basque tale. Juan de Kalais, the son of a widow, sets off as a merchant, but sells his cargo and ship to pay the debts of a corpse, which is being dragged about on a dung-heap. On his return, his mother is angry. Again he goes on a voyage, but

[1] From Gascony, like *III.*, *IV.*, and *V.*

[2] The portraits are not displayed on the ship, but on Jean's carriage,—a curious deviation.

with a very poor ship, and is compelled by an English captain to ransom a beautiful maiden with all his cargo. The hero's mother is again angry at this seemingly bad bargain, but she does not forbid his marrying the girl. Juan is now sent to Portugal by his wife with a portrait on a flag, a handkerchief, and a ring. At the same time she tells him that she has been called Marie Madeleine. When the King of Portugal sees the portrait, he sends the hero back with a general to fetch Marie, who is his daughter. The general pitches Juan overboard and goes for the princess, whom he persuades to marry him after seven years. At the end of that time, a fox comes to Juan on an island, where he has lived, and bargains to rescue him for half of all he has at present and will have later. The hero arrives in Portugal, is recognized by the king, tells his story, and has the general burned. After a year the fox appears and demands payment, but, when Juan is going to divide his child, it says that it is the soul of the dead man whom he buried long before.

The two variants are chiefly peculiar in that they introduce a new element into the compound,—*The Thankful Beast.* This substitution of some beast for the ghost has been encountered twice before[1] in connection with *Jewish* and *Servian IV.*, and must receive special treatment later on.[2] For the present it is sufficient to remark the variation from all other forms of *Jean de Calais* except *X.*[3] In both *II.* and *VII.* Jean makes two journeys,[4] as in *III.*, *IV.*, and *V.*, as against *I.* and *VI.* The attitude of the parent differs widely in the two. The maiden whom the hero marries is a Portuguese princess, which is the prevailing form of the tale. The

---

[1] See pp. 27 and 57.   [2] See chapter vii.   [3] See pp. 104 f.

[4] *II.* is the only version which has Jean make his first two voyages on land, a trait which contradicts the general testimony of the tales throughout the chapter.

portrait is also found in each, and both state the time of Jean's exile as seven years. *II.* differs from all the other versions in placing the later adventures of the story at Calais rather than at the court of the heroine's father. In *II.*, as in *VI.*, the ghost announces himself at the first meeting, which is undoubtedly a modification of the original story. Thus the two forms are sufficiently independent of one another, in spite of their common use of an animal as the hero's friend.

Jean de Calais VIII., though like *VI.* from a Breton source, differs from all the other variants, chiefly in transposing the burial and the ransom. Jean Carré, sent out by his godmother as a sea-captain, ransoms an English princess with her maid, and marries the former. After two years, when a son has been born to them, Jean goes on another voyage, and adorns the stern of his vessel with portraits of his wife, the child, and the maid, which he is begged to show while anchored at London. He does so, and is received by the king as a son-in-law. One day he sees a poor debtor's body dragged along the street, pays the debts, and has it buried. He then sets out with a fleet to seek his wife, and is cast overboard by a Jew, who is the pilot; but he is saved by a supernatural man, who carries him to a green rock in the sea. The princess refuses to go to England when the fleet arrives, and is wooed by the Jew so persistently that after two years she promises him marriage. At this juncture Jean, who has been asleep during the whole interval, is awakened by his rescuer and carried over the sea, where the man explains that he is the ghost of the debtor. Jean is first recognized by his little son, the Jew is burned by the *gendarmes*, and all ends well.

The transposition mentioned above is clearly a change due to the individual narrator or some local predecessor, since everywhere else the burial takes place before the ransom. The mention of a Jew as traitor is also peculiar and unreasonable, since no motive for his action appears until later, and then incongruously. The variant is likewise defective in not having any bargain between the ghost and the hero. In other respects it is normal save in minor details. As in *V.*, the heroine is made an English princess, which occurs nowhere else. On the whole the version is picturesque, but defective.

Jean de Calais IX. is unique in certain features, though in most respects normal. It is from Asturia in Spain. Juan de Calais goes out into the world to seek his fortune with a single peseta as his store. This he gives to bury a corpse, and proceeds. In a certain kingdom he attracts the notice of a princess, who marries him after considerable opposition. When the wedding is over, he takes his wife to seek his father's blessing, but is cast off the ship by a former suitor of the lady, her cousin. He is carried to an island by invisible hands, where he lives until a phantom bargains to take him to court for half of what he gets by his marriage. He arrives on the day of the princess's wedding. He is recognized by the king, who puts to his guests a parable of an old key found just when a new one has been made, while the suitor flees. On the following night, when Juan is dejected at the thought of giving up half his son, the phantom appears and releases him from his agreement, explaining its identity.

Juan wins the gratitude of the dead man, and obtains his bride in this version on a single journey, as in *I.* and *VI.*, but its chief peculiarity is the manner in which he gets his wife, with the sequel that the couple set out to seek his father instead of hers. The ransom is replaced by a romantic but more natural wooing, while the ghost appears somewhat unusually *in propria persona.* One of the oddest traits in the whole version is the parable of the key, by which the king introduces the

hero to the assembled guests. This will be encountered
again in *Breton VII.*

In *Jean de Calais X.*, finally, a Wallon variant, appear
certain interesting changes in the fabric. The King of
Calais sent his son Jean to America to trade, but the
prince was shipwrecked on the coast of Portugal, and
there ransomed and rescued a corpse, which was being
dragged through the streets because the man had died
in debt. The king scolded his son for wasting so much
money, but the next year sent him to Portugal to trade.
There he encountered brigands, who had captured the
king's daughter with her maid, and ransomed them. On
returning to Calais with his bride, he was ill received,
and resolved to go back to Portugal. A young lord of
Calais accompanied them and threw Jean into the sea,
while he took the princess onward and obtained from
her a promise of marriage in a year. Happily Jean
found a plank by which he reached an island, where a
crow fed him every day. At the end of a year he promised the crow half his blood for rescue, and was taken
to Portugal by a flock of crows. There he was recognized, and the traitor hanged. One day the crow appeared
and demanded the fulfilment of the promise. Jean was
about to slay his son, when the bird explained its identity
with the ghost of the dead man.

This is the only version which makes Jean a prince ;
and it is curious that the change should occur in a tale
from a region not very remote from Calais. Most of
the events of the tale take place in Portugal, however,
which is an extension of the ordinary appearance of that
country as the home of the heroine. The most striking
peculiarity of the version is the home of the traitor, who
is a lord of Calais instead of Portugal. All mention of
signs is lacking, which is doubtless due to the changes
just mentioned. In the matter of the appearance of the
ghost as an animal the variant allies itself with *II.* and

VII., though it has no special likeness to them in other respects.

Basque II. is like *Gaelic*[1] in general outline. Juan Dekos is sent out with a ship to complete his education. He pays all that he gets for his cargo to ransom and bury the corpse of a debtor. His father is not pleased, but sends him out again. This time he uses all his money to ransom eight slaves, seven of whom he sends to their homes, but carries one home with him. His father is still more angry, and casts him off; but Juan has a portrait of Marie Louise painted for the figure-head of his ship, and sets off with her for her own land. The lame mate pitches him overboard, and carries the lady to her father's dwelling-place, where he is to marry her after a year and a day. Juan is saved by an angel and placed on a rock. On Marie's wedding-day the angel returns, and offers to take the hero to his bride for half of the child that will be born. The angel was the soul of the dead man. So Juan arrives in time, is recognized by a handkerchief, and tells his story, which causes the burning of the mate. After a year the angel comes for his half of the babe, but when Juan starts to divide it stays his hand.

Webster, the collector of this tale, noticed[2] its similarity to *Gaelic,* especially in the name of the hero, and surmised that the Basques must have borrowed it from the Celts in some way. The theory is tenable, though a comparison of the two variants shows that the Basques must either have borrowed it in a form considerably different from the Highland tale as we have it, or have altered the details largely. The first part of the story is entirely different; the hero goes on two voyages in *Basque II.,* one only in *Gaelic;* the lady goes with the hero immediately in the former, he returns for her in the latter; the treachery and the signs are different; the

---

[1] See pp. 85 f.   [2] P. 146.

ghost appears as an angel instead of a human being in *Basque*; and the promised division concerns the wife and three sons in *Gaelic*, a single babe in *Basque*. Thus, apart from the title, there is little to substantiate Webster's theory. The differences are certainly more important than those between any two versions of *Jean de Calais*. In some particulars, like the voyages and the portrait on the ship, *Basque* is more nearly normal, while in others, like the account of the treachery and the appearance of the ghost, *Gaelic* conforms to the ordinary form. Certainly *Basque II.* is to be regarded as a fairly close relative of *Lithuanian II.* and *Jean de Calais.*

In *Breton VII.* a normal form appears, though with some embroidery of details. A merchant's son, Iouenn Kerménou, goes out with his father's ship to trade. He pays the greater part of the proceeds of the cargo to ransom and bury the corpse of a debtor, which dogs are devouring. On his way home he gives the rest of his money to ransom a princess, who is being carried to a ravaging serpent, which has to be fed with a royal princess every seven years. He is cast off by his father when he reaches home, but is supported by an aunt and enabled to marry his lady. After a son has been born to them, he is sent out by an uncle on another ship, which by his wife's counsel has the figure of himself and herself with their child carved on the prow. He comes to her father's realm, and after some misunderstanding is sent back with two ministers of state for the princess. While returning with her, he is pushed overboard by the first minister, who is an old suitor for the lady's hand, but swims ashore on a desert island. The wife goes to court, and after three years consents to marry the minister. All this time Iouenn lives alone on his rock, but at the end is greeted by the ghost of the man whose body he buried, which appears in a very

horrible form.   On condition of giving in a year and a
day half of what he and his wife possess, he is taken to
court by this being, where he is recognized by means of
a gold chain, which the princess had given him.   At
the wedding feast, which takes place that day, the wife
recounts a parable of how she has found the old key of
a coffer just as a new one was ready, brings in Iouenn,
and has the minister burned.   At the end of a year and
a day comes the ghost, and demands half of the child
(the older one has died) that has been born to them.
As the hero reluctantly proceeds to divide the child, the
ghost stops him, praises his fidelity, and disappears.

It will be seen that this variant does not differ in
essentials from those previously summarized, though its
details exactly coincide with none of them.   The order
of events is normal, very like that of *Lithuanian II.*, for
example, yet it has marks of peculiarity.   Chief among
these are the events connected with the ransom of the
lady and the parable by which she introduces her long
lost husband to court.   The first is a trait borrowed
from the *Perseus and Andromeda* motive,[1] the second
is the same as the riddle in *Jean de Calais IX.*[2]   How
this latter feature should happen to appear in these two
widely separated variants and nowhere else I am not
wise enough to explain.

Simrock I. introduces still another complication in the
way of compounds.   A merchant's son on a journey
secures proper burial for a black Turkish slave, thereby
using all his money.   His father is angry with him on
his return.   On his second voyage he ransoms a maiden
and is cast off by his father when he reaches home.
The young couple live for a time on the proceeds from
the sale of the wife's handiwork, but after a little set off
to the court of her father, who is a king.   On the way

[1] See *The Legend of Perseus*, E. S. Hartland, 1896, volume iii.
[2] See p. 103 above.

they meet one of the king's ships, and go aboard. The hero is cast into the sea by the captain, but is saved by a black fellow and brought back to the ship. Again he is cast overboard. When the princess arrives at home, she agrees to marry whoever can paint three rooms to her liking. The hero, meanwhile, is again saved by the black man, and in return for the promise of his first child on its twelfth birthday he is given the power of obtaining his wishes. After a year and a day he is taken to court by his friend, where by wishing he paints the three rooms, the third with the story of his life. So he is recognized. On the twelfth birthday of his first child the black man comes to him and is offered the boy, but instead of taking him explains his identity.

As far as *The Grateful Dead, The Ransomed Woman,* and the sacrifice of the child are concerned, this follows the normal course of events, except perhaps as to the child, of actually dividing which there is no question. Like *Lithuanian II., Jean de Calais III., IV., V.,* and *X., Basque II.,* and *Norwegian I.,* it makes the hero and heroine set out for her father's court together and of their own free will.[1] The colour of the thankful dead is a peculiar trait. Yet the element which complicates the question, as mentioned above, is the feat by which the hero obtains his wife. If I am not mistaken, this allies the variant on one side with stories of the type of *The Water of Life,* where the bride is gained by the performance of some task obviously set as impossible. The questions involving the relations of such motives with *The Grateful Dead* will occupy the next chapter, so that it needs simply to be mentioned at this point.

In *Simrock II.* a miller's son goes with merchandise to England. In London he pays all his money for the debts and the burial of a poor man. He is again sent to England by his father, and this time he gives his

---

[1] In *Jean de Calais IX.* they set out together, but to the hero's home.

whole ship to ransom a beautiful maiden. When he returns with her, he is cast off by his father, marries the girl, and lives on what she makes by her needle. He takes a piece of her embroidery with him to England, where it is seen by the king and queen, whose daughter has become his wife. He is sent for her in company with a minister, who pitches him overboard and goes on for the princess, hoping to marry her. The hero swims ashore, in the meantime, and communicates with his wife by means of a dove, which also feeds him. Finally a spirit conveys him to London, after receiving the promise of half of his first child. He obtains work in the kitchen of the castle, and sends a ring to his wife, by means of which they are reunited. At the birth of their child he refuses to give the spirit half, but offers the whole instead,[1] whereupon ensues an explanation.

This variant is of the same type as *Jean de Calais II.* and *VII.*,[2] resembling the latter more than the former in details. The three are sufficiently unlike, however, to make any immediate relationship quite out of the question, even did not geography forbid. As in *Hungarian II., Oliver, Lope de Vega, Calderon, Jean de Calais V.* and *VIII.*, and *Norwegian I.*, the heroine is an English princess, a point of interest, but not of much importance.

Simrock VIII. differs from the above in only two points. The beginning states that a merchant while in Turkey pays the debts and burial expenses of a poor man. On his next voyage he buys three hundred slaves from the Emperor of Constantinople. Three of them he keeps at his home, one of whom he marries. The further adventures of the hero agree with *Simrock II.* even in names and most details, except that the hero is

---

[1] So also in *Transylvanian.* Similarly the hero offers to give all of his wife, instead of dividing her, in *Dianese, Old Swedish,* and *Old Wives' Tale.*

[2] See pp. 100-102.

recognized at the court by dropping his ring in a cup of tea, which the princess gives him to drink. It will be evident that the two tales are nearly related.

Last, but not least interesting of the versions in which the child appears, is the *Factor's Garland* or *Turkey Factor*, which must have been almost as well known in England at one time as the form of the story in *Jack the Giant-Killer*. It has no very remarkable features in its outline. A young Englishman, while acting as a factor in Turkey, pays fifty pounds to have the body of a Christian buried. A little later he pays one hundred pounds to ransom a beautiful Christian slave, and takes her back to his home, where he makes her his house-keeper. Later he sets out again, and is told by the woman to wear a silk waistcoat that she has embroidered, when he comes to the court whither he is bound. The work is recognized by her father, the emperor, and the factor sent back to fetch her. While returning with the princess, he is pushed overboard in his sleep by the captain, but swims to an island, whence he is rescued by an old man in a canoe, who bargains with him for his first-born son when three (or thirty) months old. The hero is recognized at court and marries the princess, while the captain dies by suicide. In two (or three) years the old man returns, just when the couple's son is three (or thirty) months old, and demands the child. On the hero's yielding, he explains that he is the ghost, and disappears.

Like *Gaelic*[1] and *Simrock VIII.*—the latter just discussed—this version makes the hero undergo his early adventures in Turkey. Indeed, the similarity to *Gaelic* throughout is very notable, far more so than in the case of *Basque II.*[2] The only point in which it differs materially is the division of property, which in *Gaelic* concerns the wife and the three children, in the *Factor's*

[1] See pp. 85 f. [2] See pp. 105 f.

Garland one son only. In this matter there is agreement between the present variant, *Basque II.,* and *Simrock VIII.* Despite the likeness to *Gaelic,* there is no good reason for arguing any immediate connection with that version. They stand close to one another geographically and in content, that is all; they cannot be proved to be more than near relatives in the same generation.

The variants which introduce the division of the child have now all been considered. It is necessary to turn to a few scattered specimens in which the compound, *The Grateful Dead + The Ransomed Woman,* has been joined with other material.

Bohemian is a curious and instructive example of the confusion which has resulted from welding various themes together. Bolemir, a merchant's son, is sent to sea, where he is robbed by pirates and imprisoned. He finds means to help an old man, who gives him a magic flute, and a princess, who gives him half of her veil and ring. By the aid of the flute he succeeds in winning the chief's permission to leave the island in the company of his friends. He sails with them to another island. There, at the old man's request, he strikes him on the head and buries him. He then goes home with the princess. On his second voyage he displays from his mast-head a golden standard, which the princess has made. He reaches the city of the lady's father, tells his story, and returns for the princess with the chamberlain. While they are all returning together, he is cast into the sea by the chamberlain, who takes the woman to court and obtains a promise of marriage, when a church has been built to her mind. Bolemir is saved from the sea by the ghost of the old man, and is given a wishing ring. He turns himself into an eagle and flies to court, into an old man and becomes a watchman at the church. By means of his ring he builds the structure, and paints it with the story of his life. At the wedding breakfast of the princess, who cannot longer delay the bridal, he tells his story, and so marries her.

The peculiar form of the burial in this variant will be at once evident, though the reason for it is not clear to me. Disenchantment by decapitation is a common phenomenon in folk-lore and romance;[1] but though the blow on the head, which the hero gives the old man in our tale, surely stands for beheading, it is hard to see where any unspelling process comes in. It is perhaps best to suppose the trait a confused borrowing, without much meaning as it stands. The ransoming of the woman is closely connected with the benefits done the old man. That it occurs on the same journey has been shown by the variations in *Jean de Calais* to be a matter of little consequence. With respect to the standard and the ring, by which the hero restores his wife to her father, and later to himself, the tale is perfectly in accord with the prevalent form of the compound type; and so also in regard to the rescue of the hero by the ghost. No hint is given of any agreement of division between the hero and the ghost. The chief peculiarity of the variant, however, is the means by which the heroine is won. The feat recalls *Simrock I.*,[2] even in details like the demand on the part of the bride for mural decoration. It again shows the combination of the present type with a theme akin to *The Water of Life*.

Simrock III. has several points of contact with the above. Karl, the son of an English merchant, on his first voyage to Italy pays the debts of a merchant who has died bankrupt. On his way home he buys two sisters from some pirates at an inn. His father casts him off, so he marries the older of the maidens, who tells him that she is a princess. They start for Italy

---

[1] See the paper by Kittredge, *Journal of American Folk-Lore*, xviii. 1-14, 1905.

[2] See pp. 107 f.

together, and on the way meet an Italian prince, who is a suitor for the wife's hand. The hero is cast overboard, but is brought to land by a great bird, which tells him that it is the ghost of the man whom he has buried. It directs him to go to court and give himself out as a painter. The bird again comes to him there with a dagger in its beak, and tells him to cut off its head. Unwillingly Karl obeys, and sees before him the spirit of the dead man. The ghost paints the room in which they are standing with the hero's history. So on the wedding-day of the princess with the traitor, Karl explains the meaning of the pictures and wins his bride again.

This Swabian story has preserved the decapitation [1] in much better form than *Bohemian*, though the reason for its introduction is still hard to understand. The ghost is obviously released from some spell when it is beheaded, and is thus enabled to help the hero to better advantage than before. The episode also occurs in a more logical position than in *Bohemian*. It replaces the more ordinary and normal test of the hero by the ghost. Probably the introduction of it in the two cases is sporadic, though some connection between the two is conceivable. As far as *The Grateful Dead* and *The Ransomed Woman* proper are concerned, the variant has no peculiarities of special importance, being of the type in which the hero and heroine set out for court together.[2] It contains, however, the feat by which the bride is won, in the same form as in *Simrock I.* and *Bohemian*, which is due to an alliance with the type of *The Water of Life*. Yet it differs from them in making the ghost appear first as a bird, which connects it with *Jean de Calais II., VII.,* and *X.,* and with *Simrock II.* and *VIII.,* variants that have the thankful beast playing the rôle of ghost.[3]

[1] In this connection it is cited by Kittredge in the study above mentioned, pp. 9 f.

[2] See p. 108.   [3] See p. 101.

Simrock VII., together with some other peculiarities, again has the feat of winning the bride, though it is a feat of another sort. Wilhelm catches a swan-maiden, and later releases her from an enchanted mountain by hewing trees, separating grain, and finding his wife among three hundred women. Thus by her help he breaks the spell, and carries her back home. Later they journey together to her father's court. On the way Wilhelm pays the debts of a corpse, and has it buried. They meet two officers of the king, who toss Wilhelm overboard from the ship in which they sail, but he is saved by the ghost of the dead man and brought to court. He is recognized by the princess, and proves his identity to her father by means of a ring and a handkerchief.

The most salient point here is the fact that the maiden is not ransomed at all, but instead is captured like any other swan-maiden. We have already met with the theme of *The Swan-Maiden* in combination with *The Grateful Dead* in simple form ;[1] but *Servian V.* has evidently nothing to do with *Simrock VII.*, since the part played by the borrowed motive is different in each. In the former it is introduced as the reward bestowed on the hero by the ghost, while in the latter the swan-maiden simply replaces the ransomed maiden, as is shown by the subsequent events of the story, which follow the normal order as far as she is concerned. The feats by which the hero disenchants her are essentially like those in *Bohemian, Simrock I.*, and *Simrock III.*, though they are differently placed. Probably the introduction of this new material accounts for the transposition of the ransoming and the burial, as the latter is in other respects regular. It is curious to observe that the process of changing about various features, thus begun, continued in other ways, as in the matter of the signs by which the hero is recognized by his father-in-law and his wife. These

[1] See pp. 31 f.

things go to show, however, that back of the variant must have existed the compound type in a normal form.

In *Simrock V.* the thankful beast again appears, but in a less complicated setting than in the case of *Jean de Calais II., VII.,* and *X.,* or *Simrock II., III.,* and *VIII.* A widow's son on his way home from market pays the debts of a corpse and buries it, thus using all his money. The next time he goes to market, he gives all his proceeds to ransom a maiden, whom he marries. She does embroidery to gain money, and one day holds out a piece of it to the king, who is passing. He recognizes her as his daughter, and accepts the hero as son-in-law. The young couple start back home for the widow, but on the way the servants cast the young man into the sea. He escapes, however, to an island, where he is fed by an eagle. Later the eagle declares itself to be the ghost of the dead man, and brings its benefactor to court.

Oldenburgian is a similar tale. A merchant's son while on a voyage pays thirty dollars to bury a man, and also buys a captive princess with her maid. Though ill-received by his father on his return, he marries the girl. Later he goes on another voyage, with his wife's portrait as the figure-head of his ship. This is recognized by the king, who sends him back for the princess in the company of a minister. The latter pitches him overboard, goes on for the princess, and does not tell her of her loss till they arrive at court. She finally consents to marry the traitor after five years. Meanwhile, the hero lives on an island, whither on the day appointed for the princess's bridal comes the ghost of the dead in the form of a snow-white dove. It takes him to the court, where he is recognized by a ring, a gift from his bride, which he drops into a cup that she offers him.

Of these two variants, *Oldenburgian* is much better preserved than the Tyrolese story (*Simrock V.*). The latter is dressed in a homely fashion, which probably accounts for some of the changes, since the gap between the visits to market and the romantic or miraculous features of the couple's later adventures was too wide to be easily bridged. The disappointed suitor is not mentioned, which leaves the attempt on the hero's life without motivation, and clearly indicates some loss.[1] The trait is distinctly marked in *Oldenburgian,* as are all the other events connected with *The Ransomed Woman,* though *Simrock V.* provides an entirely original reason for the voyage of the young couple,—their wish to get the hero's mother. The features concerning the rescue by the ghost and the hero's return to court are better preserved again in *Oldenburgian,* though both lack the agreement to divide, which is probably obscured as elsewhere by the prominence given the rescued woman. The most striking similarity between the two, however, lies in the fact that the ghost first appears as a bird. This clearly shows the existence of a type of *The Grateful Dead + The Ransomed Woman,* on which *The Thankful Beasts* has had some influence.

It remains to consider the general relations of the variants discussed in this chapter. The wide variety in detail of the incidents concerned with the history of the hero's wife, yet the essential uniformity which they show, would indicate clearly, for one thing, that *The Ransomed Woman* is a motive originally quite independent of *The Grateful Dead,*—that the type of story which is our present concern is a true compound. It would even be possible to reconstruct the independent theme in a form not unlike the Wendish folk-tale cited in the beginning of the chapter. The hero, while on a journey, ransoms a princess, takes her home, goes on another journey with some sign that attracts her father's notice, goes back to

---

[1] The same loss is evident in *Catalan, Spanish, Simrock I.,* and *Simrock VII.*

her and is cast into the sea by some man who hopes to marry her himself, is rescued, and returns to court to claim his bride, usually by means of a token.

The points of contact between this motive and *The Grateful Dead* would seem to be, first, the journey which the hero undertakes at the opening of the plot. It will be noted that in the compound he usually makes two voyages, burying the dead on the first and ransoming the maiden on the second, though the two are sometimes welded. The second point of contact, I take it, was the rescue of the hero. In each story he did a good act for which he was rewarded in some way. It has been shown that this reward sometimes took the form of a rescue in the simple form of *The Grateful Dead*[1] and in the compound with *The Poison Maiden.*[2] What more natural than that it should lead to another combination with a story where the hero was saved from death ? The difference in the case of the latter, of course, would be that the agency of rescue was of little importance. Could *Simonides* be shown to have anything more than a literary life in mediaeval Europe, I should be inclined to think that the rescue in that tale, even though the tale itself is not necessarily connected with *The Grateful Dead* as we know the theme, might have had some influence on the union. As the matter stands, however, it is probably better to believe that the two motives were united in eastern Europe, the one being Oriental and the other of uncertain derivation. That each motive had a wife as part of the hero's reward must be taken for granted, and it must have helped to combine them.

It follows from this that the compound *The Grateful Dead* + *The Ransomed Woman* is quite independent of

[1] See p. 27 for *Jewish*.

[2] That is, the rescue of the bridegroom from the creatures which possess the bride.

the one discussed in the previous chapter, and could not have proceeded from it as Hippe thought.[1]   It would have been next to impossible for that combined type to divest itself of the features peculiar to *The Poison Maiden*, and to absorb in their place those of *The Ransomed Woman* without leaving some trace of the process.   Thus the existence of the compound as an independent growth is assured.   In this connection it is interesting to note that the rescue of the hero from drowning in consequence of an act of treachery (or from an island) occurs in all the variants of the type save four, *Transylvanian*, *Trancoso*, *Gasconian*, and *Straparola I.*,[2] but in no other version of *The Grateful Dead* as far as I know.

From this general type developed minor varieties with traits borrowed from *The Water of Life*, *The Thankful Beasts*, and *The Two Friends*, or some such tale.   Thus very complex variants arose.   The question of the connection which these subsidiary elements sustain to the central theme cannot properly be discussed until they have been seen in other combinations.   The part they play in the development of the story, it is evident, must have been a secondary one both in importance and in time.

[1] See p. 4 above.

[2] Of course this excludes the group connected with *Oliver*, which has no proper connection with the compound type.

CHAPTER VI.

THE GRATEFUL DEAD AND *THE WATER OF LIFE* OR KINDRED THEMES.

THE *märchen* known in its various forms as *The Water of Life*[1] is based on the myth which goes by the same name.[2] The myth, as has been shown quite independently by two recent investigators, Dr. Wünsche[3] and Dr. E. W. Hopkins,[4] is of Semitic origin, and is found among the traditions of the Assyrio-Babylonian cycle. It is to be distinguished from the very similar myth of *The Fountain of Youth*, which apparently originated in India.[5] The latter concerns the magic properties of the " water of rejuvenation "; the former in its uncontamin-

[1] The most adequate treatment of the motive yet published is by August Wünsche, *Die Sagen vom Lebensbaum und Lebenswasser*, 1905, pp. 90-104. This is the same study which had previously been printed in the *Zts. f. vergleichende Litteraturgeschichte*, 1899, N.F. xiii. 166-180, but is furnished with a new introduction and a few additional illustrations. Dr. Wünsche's monograph, thoroughgoing amd conclusive as it is with reference to the myths of the Tree of Life and the Water of Life, leaves much to be desired as an account of the folk-tale based on the latter belief. He himself says in his preface, p. iv : " Man sieht auch daraus, dass es sich um Wanderstoffe handelt, an die sich immer neue Elemente ankristalliert haben." These elements he has not studied with any degree of completeness. Thus, for example, he does not use Cosquin's valuable contributions in *Contes populaires de Lorraine*, i. 212-222, which would have given him valuable assistance. The theme yet awaits definitive treatment.

[2] See Wünsche, p. 92.   [3] P. 71.

[4] " The Fountain of Youth," *Journal of the American Oriental Society*, xxvi. 1st half, 19 and 55.

[5] Hopkins, pp. 19, 42, 55, etc.

ated form, at least, deals with water which cures, revivifies, or revitalizes. The two have been frequently confused, not only in popular tradition of all ages, but in critical writings of contemporary date as well. It is the great merit of Professor Hopkins' article, to which reference has been made, that their essential difference in origin and character is clearly marked. Though he makes no pretence that his study of *The Fountain of Youth* is definitive, he has broken ground which sadly needed the plough, and incidentally has thrown light upon *The Water of Life*.

The myth which is properly known by this name is intimately connected in origin and development with that of *The Tree of Life*,[1] which finds expression in the legends of the Cross. In the words of Dr. Wünsche:[2] "Wie wir aus den kosmogonischen und theogonischen Mythen und Sagen der Völker das Rauschen des Lebensbaumes vernehmen, durch dessen Früchte sich Götter und Menschen ihre ungeschwächte Lebenskraft und ewige Jugendfrische erhalten, so nicht minder das Sprudeln einer Quelle des Lebenswassers, die Leben schafft und zu Ende gehendes oder bereits erloschenes Leben wieder zu neuem Sein erweckt." Both myths are Semitic, and both have profoundly influenced Christian doctrine. It is with the "water of life," however, that we are immediately concerned, and with that only as it has found embodiment in a widely disseminated and variously modified tale. Whence this *märchen* came we must presently inquire, in order to reach some conclusion as to the point in space and time where it joined *The Grateful Dead*, but we must first fix its essential traits.

Owing to the complex variations which the tale

---

[1] Wünsche, p. iii : " Es sind altorientalische Mythen, die in alle Kulturreligionen übergangen sind. Zeit und Ort haben ihnen ein sehr verschiedenes Gepräge gegeben, der Grundgedanke ist derselbe geblieben."

[2] P. 71. See also Hopkins, p. 55.

presents in its various combinations with really foreign themes, there is great difficulty in getting at the outline of the original story or even the characteristics common to all the known variants. To do this satisfactorily would require a searching and detailed study, which it is impossible to undertake here,—an examination with *The Water of Life* as the point of attack. It is possible, however, to arrive at a rough sketch of the theme.

" Dans tous ces contes," says Cosquin, in his notes on *The Water of Life,*[1] " trois princes vont chercher pour leur père l'eau de la vie ou un fruit merveilleux qui doit le guérir, et c'est le plus jeune qui réussit dans cette entreprise. Dans plusieurs . . . les deux aînés font des dettes, et ils sont au moment d'être pendus, quand leur frère paie les créanciers (dans des contes allemands et dans les contes autrichiens, malgré l'avis que lui avait donné un hermite, un nain ou des animaux reconaissants, de ne pas acheter de 'gibier de potence'). Il est tué par eux ou, dans un conte allemand (Meier, no. 5), jeté dans un grand trou ; mais ensuite il est rappelé à la vie dans des circonstances qu'il serait trop long d'expliquer."

Dr. Wünsche's summary is somewhat different :[2] " Gewöhnlich handelt es sich um einen König und seine drei Söhne. Der König leidet an einer schlimmen Krankheit, von der ihn kein Arzt zu heilen vermag. Da wird ihm durch irgendeine Gelegenheit die Kunde, dass er von seinem Siechtum durch das Lebenswasser eines fernen Landes befreit werden könne. Aus Liebe zu ihrem Vater machen sich die drei Söhne nacheinander auf den Weg, das Lebenswasser zu holen. Doch die beiden ältesten erliegen den auf dem Wege ihnen begegnenden Versuchungen, nur der jüngste ist wegen seiner Standhaftigkeit und Bescheidenheit so glücklich, es zu erhalten. Ein Riese, ein Zwerg, ein alter Mann oder ein alte Frau

---

[1] *Contes populaires de Lorraine*, i. 213.   [2] Pp. 90 f.

sind ihm zur Auffindung der Wunderquelle behilflich, indem sie ihm guten Rat erteilen und ihm sagen, wie er es anzufangen und wovor er sich in acht zu nehmen habe. Hier und da greifen auch dienstbare Tiere, Vierfüssler, Vögel und Fische hilfreich ein, indem sie dem Jünglinge genau die Örtlichkeit des Wassers angeben, oder auch selbst ihn mit Schnelligkeit dahin bringen. Die Lebensquelle sprudelt in einem Berge, der sich nur zu gewissen Zeiten, gewöhnlich gegen Mittag oder Mitternacht von 11–12 Uhr öffnet. Im berge steht in der Regel in einem prächtigen Garten ein versunkenes Schloss, das die grossen Schätze und Kostbarkeiten birgt, durch deren Anblick der Eintretende geblendet wird. In einem Gemache des Schlosses wieder ruht auf einem Bett eine Jungfrau von wunderbarer Schönheit, die später als Prinzessin hervortritt und den Prinzen, der durch das Schöpfen des Lebenswassers sie von ihrem Zauber gelöst hat, zum Gemahle heischt. Der Prinz hat nur kurze Zeit bei ihr geruht oder ihr einen flüchtigen Kuss auf die Lippen gedrückt. In vielen Fällen wird der Eingang zur Quelle von einem Drachen oder einem anderen Ungeheuer bewacht, die erst aus dem Wege geräumt werden müssen. Es kostet einen schweren Kampf. Auf dem Heimweg trifft der jüngste Königssohn gewöhnlich mit seinen älteren Brüdern wieder zusammen, die ihr Leben durch tolle Streiche verwirkt haben und die er vom Tode loskauft. Zuweilen sind aber die Brüder durch ihre Unbedachtsamkeit in schwarze Steine verwandelt worden und liegen am Abhange des Zauberberges, oder stehen als Marmorsäulen auf demselben, oder sind infolge ihres Hochmutes in einen tiefen Abgrund eingeschlossen. Auch in diesem Zustande werden sie durch den jüngsten Bruder bald durch das geschöpfte Wasser des Lebens, bald auf seine Bitten hin wieder ins Leben gerufen. Vereint reisen sie nun mit ihrem Bruder nach Hause zum Könige. Unterwegs

aber erfasst die Beiden Falschen Neid und Missgunst,
weil ihr Bruder allein in den Besitz des Lebenswasser
gelangt ist und sie sich vergeblich darum gemüht haben.
Daher vertauschen sie das Lebenswasser, während der
Bruder schläft, mit gewöhnlichem Wasser und eilen nun
voraus und machen mit dem erbeuteten Trank den
kranken König gesund, oder sie erscheinen nach der
Ankunft des Bruders, dessen vertauschtes Wasser den
König nur noch elender gemacht hat. Dabei raunen sie
dem Könige heimlich ins Ohr, dass der jüngere Bruder
ihn habe vergiften wollen, infolgedessen dieser vom
Könige verbannt oder gar zum Tode verurteilt wird.
Derselbe lebt nun längere Zeit zurückgezogen in einer
untergeordneten Stellung, bis endlich durch die von ihm
entzauberte Prinzessin seine Unschuld an den Tag
kommt."

Dr. Wünsche gives as subsidiary types stories where a
princess wishes the magic water for herself, and, when
her two brothers fail to return with it, goes on a quest
which results in obtaining the water and releasing the
enchanted brothers ; where a mother and son are the
chief actors; where a bird, or fruit, or the water of
death is substituted for the water of life ; and where
thankful beasts appear. All of these elements and
more appear in the accessible variants, yet not all of
them can be said rightly to represent *The Water of
Life* as such. The basal traits of the story are much
more simple than Dr. Wünsche would have us believe.
They do not include, for example, the wonderful companions whom the hero finds nor the adventures with
the enchanted princess, since these are in reality traits of
originally separate themes, as will presently be shown.[1]

On the other hand, Cosquin's outline seems to me
defective in two ways. First, he does not recognize that
there existed in the original theme some reward due the

[1] See pp. 125-127 below.

hero for his constancy and intelligence in the pursuit of his quest. *A priori* this conclusion would be expected from the general manner of folk-tales, and as a matter of fact it appears in all the versions which have come to my attention. The reward almost always takes the form of a princess, though the manner in which she is won varies very greatly. In the second place, Cosquin seems to regard *The Golden Bird* as a theme quite independent of *The Water of Life*.[1] This, I think, is to lose sight of the essential likeness between the two tales, despite their difference of introduction. As Dr. Wünsche notes,[2] not only a bird, but a fruit or the water of death may be substituted for the usual object of the quest. Indeed, certain variants have more than one of these magical forces.[3] To be sure, this superfluity of riches doubtless results from the fusion of subsidiary types, but none the less it points to the original unity of the central theme, which is all that I wish to suggest.

From this discussion we emerge with an outline of *The Water of Life* in something like the following form: A sick king has three sons, who go out to seek some magical water (or bird, or fruit) for his healing. The two older sons fall by the way into some misfortune due to their own fault; but the youngest, not without aid of one sort or another from beings with supernatural powers, succeeds in the quest and at the same time wins a princess as wife. While returning, he rescues his brothers, and is exposed by their envy and ingratitude to the loss of all he has gained (sometimes even of his

---

[1] Pp. 212-214. He regards the story in Wolf, *Hausmärchen*, p. 230, as linking the two.

[2] P. 91. Cosquin, it will be noted, makes the fruit an alternative of the water of life.

[3] For example, "The Baker's Three Daughters" in Mrs. M. Carey's *Fairy Legends of the French Provinces*, 1887, pp. 86 ff., unites the water of life with both the magical apples and the bird.

life). In the end, however, he comes to his own either because the cure cannot be completed without him or because his wife brings the older princes to book.

This summary I should be unwilling to have considered as anything more than a tentative sketch, since a systematic study of the material may bring to light certain features which I have overlooked.[1] It will, however, serve its purpose here.

This simple form of *The Water of Life* is not that with which *The Grateful Dead* has combined. Indeed, the opinion that this union was secondary to that of *The Grateful Dead* with *The Poison Maiden* and *The Ransomed Woman*[2] is strengthened by the fact that it is found with both of these compound types, and that *The Water of Life* almost invariably appears in a somewhat distorted form. In point of fact, the latter tale seems to have lent itself with remarkable facility to combination with other themes. Thus it is frequently found mixed with *The Skilful Companions*[3] (both with

---

[1] The need of such a study may be shown by stating that, while Wünsche has treated about thirty variants, I know at present of something like four times that number.

[2] See p. 118 above.

[3] This well-known *märchen* has been treated by various scholars, most recently by G. L. Kittredge, in *Arthur and Gorlagon* (*Studies and Notes in Philology and Literature*, viii.) 1903, pp. 226 f., from whom I take the liberty of transcribing the following references, some of which would otherwise be unknown to me. In note 2 to p. 226 he says: "See Benfey, *Das Märchen von den* 'Menschen mit den wunderbaren Eigenschaften,' *Ausland*, 1858, pp. 969 ff. (*Kleinere Schriften* II. iii. 94 ff.); Wesselofsky, in Giovanni da Prato, *Il Paradiso degli Alberti*, 1867, I. ii. 238 ff.; d'Ancona, *Studj di Critica e Storia Letteraria*, 1880, pp. 357-358; Köhler-Bolte, *Ztsch. des Ver. f. Volkskunde*, vi. 77; Köhler, *Kleinere Schriften*, i. 192 ff., 298 ff., 389-390, 431, 544; ii. 591; Cosquin, *Contes pop. de Lorraine*, i. 23 ff.; Crane, *Italian Popular Tales*, p. 67; Nutt, in MacInnes, *Folk and Hero Tales*, pp. 445 ff.; Laistner, *Rätsel der Sphinx* ii. 357 ff.; Steel, *Tales of the Punjab*, pp. 42 ff.; Jurkschat, *Litauische Märchen*, pp. 29 ff.; etc." A peculiarly interesting specimen is that in Bladé, *Contes pop. de la Gascogne*, 1886, iii. 12-22. See also

and without *The Grateful Dead*), *The Lady and the Monster*,[1] and *The Thankful Beasts*.

The reason for the existence of the compounds just mentioned is not far to seek. With *The Skilful Companions*[2] there is a ready point of contact in the hero's need for aid in the accomplishment of his quest, another in the circumstance that three or more companions set out together with a common end in view, and still another in the fact that a maiden is rescued by them. To *The Lady and the Monster*, at least in those variants where *The Grateful Dead* appears, *The Water of Life* has the necessary approach in the rôle of the lady herself. As for *The Thankful Beasts*, their appearance at opportune

Luzel, *Contes pop. de Basse-Bretagne*, 1887, iii. 296-311 ; Carnoy and Nicolaides, *Traditions pop. de l'Asie Mineure*, 1889, pp. 43-56 ; and Goldschmidt, *Russische Märchen*, 1883, pp. 69-78.

[1] So I venture to call the story of the woman, who through enchantment or her own bad taste is the mistress of an ogre or some other monster. She is rescued by a hero, who is able to solve the extraordinary riddles or to accomplish the apparently impossible tasks which she sets him at the advice of the monster, after other suitors have perished in the attempt. See Kittredge, *Arthur and Gorlagon*, p. 250 (note to p. 249) ; Wesselofsky, *Arch. f. slav. Phil.* vi. 574. A good specimen tale is "The Magic Turban" in R. Nisbet Bain's *Turkish Fairy Tales*, 1901, pp. 102-111.

[2] Kittredge thus summarizes the tale (*work cited*, p. 226): "Three or more brothers (or comrades) are suitors for the hand of a beautiful girl. While her father is deliberating, the girl disappears. The companions undertake to recover her. One of them, by contemplation (or by keenness of sight), finds that she has been stolen by a demon (or dragon) and taken to his abode on a rock in the sea. Another builds a ship by his magic (or possesses a magic ship) which instantly transports them to the rock. Another, who is a skilful climber, ascends the castle and finds that the monster is asleep with his head in the maiden's lap. Another, a master thief, steals the girl without waking her captor. They embark, but are pursued by the monster. One of the companions, an unerring shot, kills the pursuer with an arrow. The girl is restored to her parents." This analysis would not hold for all variants, even when uncompounded (*e.g.* Grimm, *Kinder- und Hausmärchen*, No. 71, "Sechse kommen durch die ganze Welt") but a better could scarcely be made without a systematic study of the type. As Kittredge notes, the companions are not at all constant in number and function.

moments when the heroes of folk-tales need assistance is too frequent to require justification in any particular case. It is with such combinations as these, intricate and involved, that many variants of *The Grateful Dead* are found joined. Sometimes one element, sometimes another, predominates, so that the threads which unite them are hopelessly snarled. Sometimes *The Water of Life* is lost in the entanglement, or only appears as a distorted trait, while *The Skilful Companions* or *The Lady and the Monster* come out more clearly. Through this labyrinth we must painfully take our way, exercising what caution we can. The present guide recognizes the danger of losing the road and does not pretend to more than a rough and ready knowledge of the wilderness. Accordingly, he undertakes only to conduct the curious wayfarer by the least difficult of the paths that traverse it.

Let us first consider the tales into which *The Poison Maiden* and *The Ransomed Woman* do not enter, which have only *The Grateful Dead* + *The Water of Life* or some kindred theme. These include *Maltese, Polish, Hungarian I., Rumanian II., Straparola II., Venetian, Sicilian, Treu Heinrich,* and *Harz II.* They are as widely different in their characteristics as in their sources.

Maltese has the following form : The three sons of a king successively go out in search of a bird, the song of which will make their father young. The elder two lose their all by gambling with a maiden in a palace by the way. The youngest brother pays four thousand pounds sterling to bury properly a man who has been dead eight months. He is warned against the maiden by a ghost, and so wins all from her (by using his own cards), thus rescuing his brothers. When he comes to the castle, the ghost again appears, and tells him to take the bird that he finds in a dirty cage. On the way back he is thrown overboard from the steamboat by his brothers, but is saved by the ghost, who appears in the form of a rock with a tree on it. He is rescued by another steamer, and comes home in rags, where he is recognized by the bird, which has hitherto refused to sing. The brothers are banished.

According to the *Polish* story, a poor scholar pays his all for the burial of a corpse lying maltreated by the way. Later he goes to sleep under an oak, and on awaking finds his purse full of gold. He is robbed of this while crossing a stream, by some scoundrels who cast him into the water; but he is rescued by the ghost of the dead man, who appears in the form of a plank and gives him the power of turning himself into a crow, a hare, or a deer. He becomes a huntsman to a king, whose daughter lives on an inaccessible island. In her castle is a sword with which a man could overcome the greatest army. When war threatens, the king offers the princess to any man who can obtain the sword. By means of his power of metamorphosis the hero carries her a letter and wins her love. When he exhibits his magical powers, she cuts off a bit of the fur, or a feather, from each creature into which he turns. With the sword he then starts back to court, but on the way he is shot by a rival and robbed of the sword and a letter from the princess. He lies in the way in the form of a dead hare till the war is ended and the rival is about to marry the princess, when he is revived and warned by the ghost. At court he is recognized by the princess, who proves his tale by having him turn into various shapes and fitting the samples which she has taken.

In *Hungarian I.* a soldier gave all he had to an old beggar, who in turn gave him the power to change at will into a dove, a fish, or a hare. He took service with a king, and one day was sent back to the castle for a magic ring. There he met the princess, and exhibited to her his powers of metamorphosis, permitting her to pull two feathers, take eight scales, and cut off his tail. While running back to the king in the form of a hare, he was shot by an envious comrade, who took the ring and was rewarded. The hero was restored to life by the old beggar, and returned to the castle, where he was brought to the princess. She succeeded in proving the truth of his story by means of the feathers, the scales, and the tail, which she had so fortunately preserved.

Rumanian II., though changed into legendary form, does not differ greatly from the two variants just cited. A shepherd boy gave his one sheep to Christ, when He asked for food. In return, he received a knife with three blades. Later he took service with a man, with whom he entered the army of the emperor. One day the monarch found that he had forgotten his ring, and promised half his kingdom to anybody who could bring it to him from the palace within twenty-four hours. By means of his magical knife the hero changed into a hare, obtained the emperor's ring as well as one from the princess's own hand, and returned to the army. There he was met by his master, who plundered him, threw him into a spring, and went to the emperor for reward. When the battle was over and all had returned to the capital, the princess said that the man who was presented as her bridegroom was not he to whom she gave the ring. Meanwhile, Christ had rescued the hero from the spring and sent him to the palace in the form of a fox with his ring in a basket. The princess recognized from the token that he was her true bridegroom, and brought him to the emperor.

Straparola II. introduces certain new elements to our notice. A king's son releases a wild man, whom his father has incarcerated, in order to get back an arrow that the man has taken from him. The man is really a disappointed lover, who had given himself up to a savage life. The boy's mother, in fear of the king, sends him

I

away in the care of two faithful servants, with whom he
lives in obscurity till he is sixteen years old.   Covetous
of his wealth, they are about to kill him, when the wild
man, transformed into a splendid knight by a grateful
fairy, joins them.   They go to a beautiful city called
Ireland, which is devastated by a ferocious horse and an
equally savage mare.   The traitorous servants plot to
destroy the prince by giving out, first, that he has boasted
that he can overcome the horse, and, second, the mare.
By the advice of his unknown friend and the help of
the latter's fairy horse, he accomplishes these labours.
He is told by the king that he may have one of his
daughters in marriage, if he can tell which has hair of
gold.   He is told by his companion that a hornet, which
he has released, will appear at the test and fly three
times around the head of the princess whom he is to
choose.   The man explains at the same time the cause
of his benevolence,—gratitude because by him he has
been delivered from death.   The prince is thus enabled
to pick out the princess with golden hair, and is married
to her, while his companion receives the sister.

In the *Venetian* tale, again a peculiar variant, twelve
brothers seek twelve sisters as wives.   Eleven of them
go out at first, and are turned to stone.   The youngest
brother sets out after a year, and on the way has a
poor dead man buried.   Later, when he has saved his
eleven brothers, they become envious, and throw him into
a well.   The thankful dead man then comes, draws him
out with a cord, and explains who he is.   The hero
proceeds to his home and tells his story.

Sicilian is more extended but less difficult to place.
The three orphaned sons of a rich man try to win the
daughter of a certain king, who has announced that he
will marry the princess to anyone who can make a ship
that will travel alike on land and water.   The eldest
and middle brothers are unsuccessful because they are

unkind to the poor who ask for work. The youngest
brother gives work to both old and young, and, when
an old man (St. Joseph) appears, makes him overseer.
After the work is done, he agrees to give half of what
he obtains to the old man, and goes with him in the
ship to court. On the way he takes in a man who is
found putting clouds in a sack, another who is bearing
half a forest on his back, another who has drunk half a
stream, another who is aiming his bow at a quail in the
underworld, and another who stands with one foot at
Catania and the other at Messina. At the court the
king refuses to give up his daughter till the hero can
send a message to the underworld and get an answer in
an hour, which he does by means of the long-strider and
the shooter; and till he can find a man who will drink
half the contents of his cellar in one day, which the
drinker easily accomplishes. The king then offers as
dowry only what one man can carry away, but he is
foiled by the man who bore half the forest on his back,
who now takes all the contents of the palace and departs
with the hero, the princess, and their companions. The
king pursues them, but is befogged by the man with the
clouds. When they arrive at home, the saint demands
his half, even of the king's daughter; but when the hero
takes his sword to divide her, he cries out that he merely
wished to test his faithfulness.

In *Treu Heinrich* a noble youth lost his property
through prodigality in tournaments. Finally he sold his
all to enter a tourney for the hand of the daughter of
the King of Cyprus, but he gave half to his faithful
follower Heinrich. After they set out for Cyprus, they
were joined by a knight, who shared the hero's hospitality
for fourteen days, agreeing to do the same in return, but
at last riding away. In destitution they arrived at
Famagust in Cyprus. While Heinrich was in the city,
the hero found a clear stone left by a bird, through which

he obtained power to become a bird. He then established himself in the city, met the princess with the result that they fell in love, and flew to her chamber as a bird. He obtained from her not only his desire but an ornament which he gave to the strange knight, who had again joined him. Later he overcame this knight in the tourney, but the latter was mistaken for himself. Again he flew to the princess, who gave him a crown, and again, after giving it to the stranger, he overcame him in a fight. The princess now gave him a helmet, which he kept; and he was proclaimed victor of the jousting. Once more he flew to the princess, and obtained from her an ornament for his helmet, made by herself. Thus he won her as wife.

In *Harz II.* our primary motive is far less obscure than in the version just summarized. A youth pays his all, thirty-eight dollars, to free a dead man from indebtedness. He goes his way, and meets a young fellow, who accompanies him. They fall in with a man bearing two trees, a man with a hat on one side, a man with a wooden leg, and a man with a blind eye. The six go together to a city, where the princess can be won only by performing feats, with the penalty of death attached to failure. The companions aid the hero by bringing water from a distant spring and by keeping a fiery furnace habitable, so that he wins the princess.

These nine variants are, it will be seen, related in very different degrees to *The Grateful Dead.* What a debased type of the *märchen* they represent is shown by the fact that in no less than five[1] the burial of the corpse, which is the most fundamental trait of the theme, has been lost. Yet for two reasons it is clear that they are really scions of the stock. In the first place, wherever the burial has been cut away, other elements of

---

[1] *Hungarian I., Rumanian II., Straparola II., Sicilian,* and *Treu Heinrich.*

the motive in its simple form have been retained. Thus in *Hungarian I.* and *Rumanian II.* the deeds of the old beggar (or Christ) make his identity with the ghost unquestionable ; in *Straparola II.*, despite its sophistication, the wild man fills the same rôle, while his explanations at the end show that the burial has been merely blurred ; in *Sicilian* both the agreement to divide and the division of the woman as a test are introduced ; and in *Treu Heinrich* there is double division in a way, since the hero divides his property with his faithful follower to begin with and afterwards agrees to an exchange of hospitality with the helpful knight, going so far as actually to give him two of the four gifts received from the princess. In the second place, certain variants without the burial are very closely allied with others which retain it,[1] as will be seen in a moment. Thus all those treated here may safely be admitted to the group.

The reader must, however, have been struck, while examining the summaries just given, with the great diversity of the residuum which would be left if the parts properly belonging to *The Grateful Dead* were taken away. Indeed, they may be separated on this score into four categories with a couple of minor divisions. *Polish, Hungarian I.*, and *Rumanian II.* are very similar in respect to these matters, having a princess who is won by the feat of obtaining something left at home by her father (this feat made possible by the power given the hero to change his form) and a treacherous rival. *Polish* has the peculiarity that the article to be obtained by the hero is a magical sword.[2] *Treu Heinrich* stands a little apart from these, since the rival does not appear

[1] Thus *Hungarian I.* and *Rumanian II.* with *Polish*, *Sicilian* with *Harz II.*

[2] Possibly a trace of some such story as *The Quest of the Sword of Light* discussed by Kittredge, *Arthur and Gorlagon*, pp. 214 ff.

and the princess is won by a tourney; yet it has the curious metamorphosis, and must be considered as having some connection. *Maltese* and *Venetian* fall together. *Venetian* has retained from *The Water of Life* only the misfortune and the treachery of the older brothers,[1] while *Maltese* keeps also the magical bird and the features naturally connected therewith. The introduction of two steamboats in the latter is a curious illustration of the ease with which popular tales change details without altering essentials. *Sicilian* and *Harz II.* again are alike, both being compounded with *The Skilful Companions,*[2] and making the winning of the princess depend on feats really accomplished by the helpers characteristic to that tale. *Straparola II.* must be placed alone, having nearly all trace of *The Water of Life* lost in the traits of *The Lady and the Monster,* with a princess won by the hero's happily directed choice.[3]

All of these features will appear again when we come to discuss variants which combine the compound types *The Grateful Dead + The Poison Maiden* or *The Ransomed Woman* with *The Water of Life.* They may, therefore, be passed over for the present, together with the question as to whether such a simple combination as *The Grateful Dead + The Water of Life* may be regarded as being the original from which the more complicated types have sprung. It is sufficient for the moment to recognize the tendency of the simpler variants to fall

[1] Since twelve brothers set out to win twelve sisters, there is probably a union here with the widespread tale of *The Brothers and Sisters.*

[2] The ship that will travel equally well on land and water is seemingly a common trait in forms of *The Skilful Companions.* See the variant cited from Bladé on p. 125, note 3. It occurs in a curious tale from Mauritius, given by Baissac, *Le Folk-lore de l'Île-Maurice,* 1888, p. 78.

[3] For examples of stories in which a king's son liberates one or more prisoners, and has the service returned in an emergency, see Child, *English and Scottish Popular Ballads,* v. 42-48.

into groups on the basis of the residuum left by subtracting traits belonging to *The Grateful Dead*.

Let us now consider the tales where a thankful beast plays the part of the grateful dead through at least a portion of the narrative, and where there is still no trace of either *The Poison Maiden* or *The Ransomed Woman*. The change of beast for ghost is so obvious and easy that the separation of these variants from the preceding appears at first sight to be of merely formal use. Yet thus considered, they may serve to define the subdivisions already noticed. Nine such versions have come to my knowledge: *Walewein, Lotharingian, Tuscan, Brazilian, Basque I., Breton IV., V., and VI.,* and *Simrock IX.* All but one are folk-tales, and that, curiously enough, an episode in a thirteenth century[1] Dutch romance translated from the French.[2]

Walewein, the variant in question, has the following form: Walewein (or more familiarly Gawain) sets forth from Arthur's court to secure a magical chessboard. He is promised it by King Wonder if only he will get the sword of rings from King Amoris, who in turn will give that up if Walewein will bring him the princess of the Garden of India. On this quest the hero mortally wounds a certain Red Knight, who prays him for Christian burial and is properly interred. He then proceeds to the castle of King Assentin, whose daughter recognizes in him the ideal knight whom she has seen in a dream. He is led under the dark river which surrounds the castle by the Fox Rogès, and wins the princess. The lovers and the fox (a prince transformed) escape by the help of the Red Knight's ghost. After many adventures they come together to the court with a chessboard, which is given up by King Wonder in exchange for the sword. Walewein is able to keep the princess for his own because of the death of Amoris.

[1] See Jonckbloet, ii. 131 ff.   [2] Paris, *Hist. litt. de la France*, xxx. 82.

Lotharingian runs as follows: A king has three sons. He sends them successively to seek the water of life. Two of them refuse to help a shepherd on the way, and rest from their search in Pekin. The third, who is deformed, aids the shepherd, and receives from him some arrows, which will pierce well whatever they strike, and a flageolet, which will make everyone dance within hearing of it. Arrived at Pekin, the humpback pays the debts of a corpse, and has it buried. He goes on till his money is exhausted. When he is about to shoot a fox one day, he is stayed by pity, and is directed by the creature to the castle where the water of life is to be found. There he is detained by an ogre, and wins battles for him by the aid of the magical arrows. There is a princess in the castle, who refuses to marry the ogre. The hero makes her dance, and obtains from the ogre as recompense the promise of whatever he wishes. He asks for the most beautiful thing there and the right to circle the castle three times. So he takes the princess, a phial of the water of life, as well as the uglier of the two mules and of the two green birds, as the fox has told him, and flees away. He meets the fox again, and is warned not to help any one in trouble. Nevertheless, he rescues his two brothers from the scaffold in Pekin, and is cast into a well by them. They go home, but are not able to heal the king. Meanwhile, the prince is saved by the fox, and is made straight of body. He goes home, and at his coming the king becomes young again, while the brothers are burned. So the prince marries the lady.

In *Tuscan* we learn that the youngest of three princes, while wandering, paid the debts of a man whose corpse was being insulted. When he had buried the man, he found himself without a farthing, and so slept in the forest. In the morning he was greeted by a hare (*lieprina*) with a basket of food in its mouth. He took this gladly, and reflected that the creature must be the soul of the man whom he had buried. He then came to an inn, and took service with the host, whose beautiful daughter he soon discovered to be a princess, who had been bought while an infant. After winning her love, the hero went on into two kingdoms, where he obtained a magical purse and a wonderful horse from two ugly daughters of innkeepers. With these possessions he returned to the princess, and started with her for his home. On the way he saved from death his two older brothers, who had gone out to seek adventures at the same time as himself. They repaid the kindness by trying to drown him and by carrying the princess off home, where only by feigning illness could she frustrate their plan that she choose one of them as husband. Meanwhile, the hero was rescued from drowning by the hare, and came home. By pretending to be a physician he obtained access to the princess, was recognized, and then revealed himself to his father.

The *Brazilian* tale is brief but not unusual in type. A prince, while seeking a remedy for his father, passes through a town and sees a corpse, which is held for debt. He pays the creditors, and has the corpse buried. Later he is met by a fox, which helps him obtain not only the remedy for his father but in addition a princess as his wife. On its last appearance the beast declares that it is the soul of the man whom he buried.

Basque I. has the following form : Three sons go out to seek a white blackbird by which their father can be healed. Two of them get into debt to the same three ladies, and, according to the custom of the land, are imprisoned. The third son resists the sirens, ransoms his brothers, and also pays the debts of a dead man, whose corpse is being maltreated. He arrives at the house of the king who has the white blackbird, and is told to get a certain young woman from another king.

He goes far on till he comes near the castle, where he meets a fox and is instructed by it to enter a certain room, in which he will find the lady dressed in poor clothing. He must have her put on good clothes, and she will sing. He follows the advice, but is interrupted, while the lady is singing, by the king of the castle, who tells him that he must get a white horse from still another king. He meets the fox again, and is instructed that, when he finds the horse with an old saddle on it, he must put on a good one, so that it will neigh. Again he follows the fox's advice, and is interrupted by people who rush in when they hear the horse neigh. From them he obtains the steed, and retraces his steps, eloping with the lady at the second king's castle and at the first king's carrying off the blackbird. On his arrival at home he is thrown into a cistern by his treacherous brothers, who take his spoil to the king. He is saved by the fox, however, which draws him out with its tail. When he comes into the presence of his father, and not till then, is the healing accomplished.

In *Breton IV.* we find again three sons of a king, who set forth to get the white blackbird and also the lady with locks of gold. Jeannot, the youngest of them, pays for the interment of a beggar on the way. Later a fox comes to him, saying that it is the soul of the poor man. It helps him procure the youth-giving blackbird and afterward the lady with the marvellous hair. He then meets his brothers, who for envy push him over a precipice, but he is saved and sent homeward by the fox.

Breton V. does not differ materially from the preceding, though it has interesting minor variations. The three sons of a king seek the bird Drédaine in its golden cage in order to cure their father. The two elder brothers go to England, and there meet jolly companions, but find no trace of the bird. The third brother, the ugly one, comes thither, is mocked and robbed by them, but goes his way. One night he lodges in a forest hut, and there finds a man's body, which the widow cannot bury for lack of money to pay the priest. He is now poor, but pays for the interment of the corpse, and proceeds. He is followed by a white fox, which instructs him how to achieve his quest. He soon reaches the castle, traverses three courts, comes to one chamber where he finds a piece of inexhaustible bread, enters a second where he gets an unfailing pot of wine and makes love to a sleeping princess, and goes on to a third where he finds a magical sword and the bird. He hastens away with his booty, guided for a time by the fox, sells his bread and his wine to innkeepers on condition that they be given up to the princess if ever she comes for them, and arrives at the city where his brothers are now in prison. He ransoms them by helping the king, and pays their debts by selling his sword. On their way home he is thrown into a well by his brothers, who take the bird to their father, but do not succeed in curing him. Meanwhile, the hero is saved by the fox, which now explains that it is the soul of the man whom he has buried, and definitely disappears. He arrives at his home as a beggar, and takes service with his father. Later the princess comes thither with the son that is the fruit of their union, and brings with her the bread, wine, and sword which she has found on the way. The bird sings, the king is healed, and the wicked brothers are executed.

Breton VI. lacks some of the interesting traits of the variant just given, but embroiders the theme with considerable grace. The three sons of a king set out to find the princess of Hungary, who has the only remedy that will cure their father. The eldest forgets his purpose, and wastes his money in rioting. The second finds him just as he is being led to death on account of debt, ransoms him, and shares his riotous pleasures. The third

brother, a humpback, goes out with little money, but on his
way procures burial for a man's corpse, which the widow
has been unable to do because of lack of money to pay
the priest. The next day a fox with a white tail meets
him, and in return for a bit of cake leads him to the
castle of a princess. There the prince resists the lady's
advances, which he suspects are derisive, and is sent to
her sister's castle, where he has the same experience.
When he arrives at the castle of the third sister, he yields
to her proposals, is given the remedy for his father and
a magical sword, and is told how to go home. On the
way he rescues his brothers from the scaffold by waving
his sword, and is robbed and thrown into a well by them.
Thence he is rescued by the fox, which comes at his
call, and before it disappears explains that it is the
ghost. Meanwhile, the older brothers have cured the
king by the water of life in a phial; so when the hero
comes home he is not believed. In a year and a day
the princess arrives there according to her promise, and
with a little son. At a feast she proclaims the truth,
cuts her husband into bits, sprinkles the heap of frag-
ments with the water of life, and marries the handsome
youth who at once arises—the humpback transformed.[1]

According to *Simrock IX.*, finally, the three sons of a
king seek the bird phœnix to cure their blind father.
The two elder enter the castle of a beautiful maiden, and
are lost; but the youngest resists the temptation, and
takes lodging at an inn. There at night he is startled
by a ghost, which tells him that it is the spirit of a man
whom the host has buried in the cellar for non-payment
of a score, and which implores his help. The youth
arranges for payment of the debt and for proper burial,
then goes his way. In the wood he meets a wolf, which
instructs him how to find the bird phœnix in a cage in

---

[1] The only instance known to me where such transformation occurs with
reference to the hero.

the magical castle, and carries him thither. Because he fails to take the worse-looking bird according to instructions, he has to get a steed as swift as wind for the lord of the castle. Again he is disobedient when told to take the worst-looking horse only, and so has to get the most beautiful woman in the world for the lord of this castle. Again he is brought by the wolf to a castle, where he obediently chooses a black maiden instead of one who is apparently beautiful. With maiden, horse, and bird he turns home. The wolf in parting from him explains that it is the ghost of the dead man, and warns him not to buy gallows flesh. When he meets his brothers on their way to be hanged, however, he forgets this, and ransoms them. In return he is nearly murdered by them and left for dead, but is rescued and healed by the wolf, and so at last reaches his destination.

In none of these nine stories is the burial of the dead, one of the two most fundamental features of our leading motive, in any way obscured. They are thus less difficult to treat than was the preceding group, in spite of the added complications introduced by the advent of the helpful animal. This creature should naturally take the rôle of the ghost, appear as the embodiment of the dead man's soul indeed ; and with but two exceptions[1] it actually fulfils the part. In those two there has been, apparently, imperfect amalgamation, so that the helper is duplicated, and the motivation obscured. In *Walewein*, a literary version, consciously adapted to the requirements of a *roman d'aventure*, this need excite no wonder. The ghost does its part properly, and the fox is merely an additional agency in the service of the hero, acting out of pure kindness of heart[2] as far as one can see. *Lotharingian*, not contented with duplicating the trait, triplicates it.

---

[1] *Walewein* and *Lotharingian*.

[2] Like the wolf in *Guillaume de Palerne*, which is likewise a transformed prince.

The fox, as in the ordinary form of *The Thankful Beasts*, helps the hero because of a benefit received ; the shepherd bestows magical gifts, as in a common type of *The Water of Life*, because of the hero's kindness ; while the dead debtor remains inactive after the burial, and plays no further part in the narrative.

As for *The Water of Life*, there are fewer complications in this group than in that where the thankful beast does not appear. In all of the variants some of the fundamental traits of the theme remain intact. In all save *Walewein* and *Brazilian* (which is a degenerate form presumably carried across the sea by Spaniards or Portuguese) the three brothers set out from home in quite the normal way. *Walewein* again lacks the water of life, which *Brazilian* retains. All the other versions, save *Tuscan*, keep this water or replace it by some other restorative agency. Two variants only fail to make the older brothers act treacherously towards the hero, these being again *Walewein* and *Brazilian*. The former thus lacks three of the essentials of the theme, the latter two. Yet since *Walewein* makes the hero win his princess by going on from adventure to adventure quite in the normal manner, and since *Brazilian* makes him obtain both water of life and princess, though with loss of interesting details, we are surely justified in placing both in this category.

It is worth our while to note in this connection that all these nine variants come from southern Europe, directly or by derivation.[1] Geographical proximity, though not sufficient in itself as a basis of classification, adds welcome confirmation to other proof in cases like this, where a small group of highly complicated tales is found to exist in neighbouring countries only. That

---

[1] *Lotharingian* comes from a region farther north than any other, since the Dutch romance is merely a translation from Old French. *Simrock IX.* is from Tyrol.

Walewein can be connected with this specialized sub-division has important bearings on the question whence the material for that romance was taken. In view of the limited territory which this form of the story has covered as a folk-tale in six hundred years, and the fact that France would be the centre of the region, it seems fair to assume that some thirteenth century French writer took a *märchen* of his own land as the basis for his work, thus elaborating with native material the adventures of a Celtic hero.

The question now arises as to what light the group just considered throws upon the variants which combine the simple theme of *The Grateful Dead* with *The Water of Life* or some such motive. It appeared, the reader will remember, that according to the elements foreign to the main motive they must be separated into four classes. Reference to these classes [1] will show that the variants with *The Thankful Beasts* are in many respects different from any one of them as far as the features peculiar to *The Water of Life*, or kindred themes, are concerned. Yet because *Maltese* and the brief *Venetian*, though otherwise transformed, are the only tales aside from these [2] that preserve the treachery of the hero's brothers, it is safe to class them together. Both *Maltese* and *Venetian* come, it will be observed, from the same general region as all the other members of the group.

Since the elements left by subtracting *The Grateful Dead* from the variants of the four categories thus discovered are very diverse, we cannot postulate a parent form from which all four classes might have sprung. Indeed, the evidence thus far obtained all points to a separate combination of already developed themes with *The Grateful Dead*. The test of this will be found in

[1] See pp. 133-135.
[2] I include all the tales treated in this chapter.

an examination of those variants of those larger compounds, which have also traces of *The Water of Life*
or some allied motive.

Turning first to such versions of the combination *The
Grateful Dead + The Poison Maiden*, we find eleven on
our list, all of which have already been summarized and
discussed in connection with the simple compound.[1]
These are *Esthonian II., Rumanian I., Irish I., Irish II.,
Irish III., Danish III., Norwegian II., Simrock X.,
Harz I., Jack the Giant-Killer,* and *Old Wives' Tale.*
Since we know definitely that *Danish III.* (the tale by
Christian Andersen) was taken from *Norwegian II.,* it
may be left out of account.   Ten variants thus remain
to be studied with reference to the subsidiary elements.

In *Esthonian II.* the hero releases a princess, who goes
with devils every night to church, by watching in the
church for three nights with three, six, and twelve candles
on successive nights.   In *Rumanian I.* the hero wins a
princess by explaining why she wears out twelve pairs
of slippers every night; and he accomplishes this by the
aid of his helper, who follows the lady in the form of a
cat, and picks up the handkerchief, spoon, and ring
which she drops in the house of the dragons.   According
to *Irish I.* the helper obtains for the hero horses of gold
and silver, a sword of light, a cloak of darkness, and a
pair of slippery shoes; he helps him keep over night a
comb and a pair of scissors, in spite of enchantment, and
finally gets the lips of the giant enchanter, so that the
hero unspells and wins the lady of his quest.   In *Irish II.*
the hero is joined by a green man (the grateful dead), a
gunner, a listener, a blower, and a strong man.   By the
aid of the first he gives his princess a pair of scissors, a
comb, and the enchanter's head ; by the aid of the others
he obtains water from the well of the western world, and
is enabled to walk over three miles of needles.   *Irish III.*

[1] See pp. 58-73.

has a helper who obtains for the hero a sword, a cloak of darkness, and swift shoes, rescues a pair of scissors, and obtains the enchanter's head, while the hero wins a race by the aid of the shoes. According to *Norwegian II.* the hero and helper get a sword, a ball of yarn, and a hat, while the latter follows the princess and rescues a pair of scissors and a ball, finally obtaining the troll's head. In *Simrock X.* the helper secures three rods, a sword, and a pair of wings, follows the princess, and learns how to answer her riddles, emphasizing his knowledge by getting the wizard's head. *Harz I.* has the helper give wings and a rod to the hero, who flies with the princess and learns to guess her riddles, cutting off the monster's head. In *Jack the Giant-Killer* Jack obtains gold, a coat and cap, a sword, and a pair of slippers for his master, follows the princess, and secures the handkerchief and the demon's head, which are requisite to the unspelling. Finally, according to *Old Wives' Tale*, the helper, while invisible, slays the conjuror, and so obtains the princess for his master.

It will at once be recognized that all of these variants are of one type as far as the traits just specified are concerned. The basal element is the hero's success in winning an enchanted princess either by accomplishing difficult feats or answering riddles. The water of life, as such, appears in only one story, *Irish II.*, and there not as the prime goal of the hero's quest, but merely as the object of a subsidiary labour. Clearly these tales not only form a group by themselves, but have in combination with *The Grateful Dead* and *The Poison Maiden* a theme which is not properly *The Water of Life.* This theme is as clearly *The Lady and the Monster*,[1] which is closely allied to *The Water of Life*, but is essentially distinct. It has already been found compounded with the simple form of *The Grateful Dead* in the somewhat

[1] See p. 126, note 1.

degenerate and literary *Straparola II.*,[1] though the method by which the enchanted princess was won in that variant was different from that given in the present group.

Within the group there are minor differences with reference to the manner of unspelling the princess, which resolve themselves either, on the one hand, into the hero's keeping or obtaining something for her, or, on the other, into his guessing the object of her thoughts. These details are not, however, of much importance for the purpose in hand, though they might become so if an attempt were made to sub-divide the group. Thus *Esthonian II.* is decidedly unusual in its treatment of the matter just mentioned. *Irish I.* has traces of the *Sword of Light*[2] and of *The Two Friends.*[3] In *Harz I.* the hero himself follows the princess instead of leaving the actual work of unspelling to the helper, as is elsewhere the case. *Irish II.*, finally, is peculiar not only in bringing in *The Water of Life*, as mentioned above, but also the motive of *The Skilful Companions*, which we have already met with in *Sicilian* and *Harz II.*[4]

Irish II. is, indeed, of great importance to our study at this point. It is in some way a link between *Sicilian* and *Harz II.* and the subdivision now under discussion. Furthermore, the fact that *Straparola II.* has some traits of *The Lady and the Monster* in common with all the members of the group under consideration shows that it can safely be placed in the same category as *Sicilian* and *Harz II.* Though the feats by which the princess is won are somewhat different in the last-named variants from the feats in *Straparola II.* on the one hand and in the compound *The Grateful Dead + The Poison Maiden + The Water of Life (The Lady and the Monster)* on the other, there can be little doubt, it seems

---

[1] See p. 134.   [2] See p. 133, note 2.

[3] See pp. 92 ff. above, and pp. 156-158 below.

[4] With the form *The Grateful Dead + The Water of Life* simply.

to me, that all of them belong together. *Irish II.* by the introduction of *The Skilful Companions* thus furnishes a clue by which the tales having the compound just mentioned may be classed with two varieties of the simple combination, and permits us to reduce the total number of categories with reference to *The Water of Life* from four to three.

Before proceeding to a general discussion of the means by which this theme was brought into connection with *The Grateful Dead* and the comparative date of the combination or series of combinations, it is necessary to examine four other versions,—those which have the form *The Grateful Dead* + *The Ransomed Woman* + *The Water of Life.* Like the group just treated, all of them have been summarized and discussed with reference to the prime features of the compound.[1] They are *Bohemian, Simrock I., Simrock III.,* and *Simrock VII.*

The elements of these variants, apart from those due to the main compound, are as follows. In *Bohemian* the hero is given a flute and a captive princess by his helper, and escapes with them from prison. Later he is cast into the sea by a rival, but is rescued by the helper and given a wishing ring. By means of this ring he turns first into an eagle and afterwards into an old man, and succeeds in winning the princess by building and painting a church. In *Simrock I.* the hero is rescued by the helper after being cast overboard by a rival, and is given the power of obtaining his wishes. Thereby he paints three rooms to the liking of the princess, and is recognized by her. *Simrock III.* differs from this only in making the helper do the painting and in having one room painted instead of three. In *Simrock VII.,* finally, the hero releases a princess by hewing trees, separating grain, and choosing his mistress among three hundred women, all without aid. Later he is rescued

[1] Pp. 107 f., 111-115.

from the sea and recognized by means of a ring and a handkerchief.

The first three of these variants clearly show in the subsidiary elements just enumerated their relationship to *The Water of Life.* They lack the quest for some magical fountain or bird, to be sure, but they preserve the quest for the lady, which is an important factor in the *märchen.* Of the three, *Bohemian* has the most extended and probably the best presentation of the details of the difficult courtship; and it gives the hero that power of metamorphosis which was noted in four variants of the type *The Grateful Dead + The Water of Life* simply. It may, therefore, on the basis of general and particular resemblance be classed with *Polish, Hungarian I., Rumanian II., and Treu Heinrich.*[1] Along with it, of course, go the briefer *Simrock I.* and *Simrock III.* There is this important difference between the two sets of tales, that in the simpler form the princess is won by the hero's success in bringing something from a distance, in the more complicated form by building and decorating. Yet the resemblance is sufficient to warrant the classification proposed.

With *Simrock VII.* the case is altogether different. There the subsidiary elements are connected with *The Lady and the Monster* rather than *The Water of Life* proper, yet not with that theme as it appears in combination with *The Poison Maiden,*[2] since in that group the hero disenchants the princess by guessing some secret, here by performing two feats of prowess or discrimination and by choosing the proper lady from a host of maidens. With *Straparola II.,* however, which has the simpler combination *The Grateful Dead + The Lady and the Monster,* the resemblance is very close,[3] as both have the happily directed choice. The complicated *Simrock VII.* thus falls into the same category with reference

[1] See pp. 133 f.   [2] See pp. 145-147.   [3] See pp. 146 f.

to this matter as *Straparola II.*, *Sicilian*, and *Harz II.*, and the group having the form *The Grateful Dead +*
The Poison Maiden + The Water of Life (*The Lady and the Monster* specifically).

A summary of our three categories will be of service in discussing their relations to one another and to the themes with which *The Water of Life* or *The Lady and the Monster* are combined.

CLASS I.
> *Polish.*
> *Hungarian I.*
> *Rumanian II.*
> *Treu Heinrich.*
> *Bohemian.*
> *Simrock I.* ⎫ (With *The Ransomed Woman*.)
> *Simrock III.* ⎭

CLASS II.
> *Sicilian.*
> *Harz II.*
> *Straparola II.*
> All recorded variants with *The Poison Maiden.*
> *Simrock VII.* (With *The Ransomed Woman*.)

CLASS III.
> *Maltese.*
> *Venetian.*
> All variants with *The Thankful Beasts.*

Class I. forms a territorially homogeneous group, all the members of it coming from eastern and central Europe. It is not altogether homogeneous in content, but preserves the theme of *The Water of Life* proper in a form where the hero wins a princess by means, among other feats, of metamorphosis. Class II. is the most widespread of all territorially, as its members come from all parts of Europe. It has instead of *The Water of Life* proper what must be regarded, in the present state of the evidence, as the closely allied theme of *The Lady and the Monster.* Class III., the most compact of all in the region that it inhabits, preserves *The Water of Life* better than any other group, though not without frequent admixture and, in many instances, the loss of some elements.

It has been stated above [1] that it would be hard to imagine such various traits coming from a single type of story. This becomes even more evident from the tabulation just made. To suppose that *The Grateful Dead* first united with *The Water of Life*, and that this compound gave rise to the varieties, as enumerated, would involve us in the direst confusion. If such were the case, how could Class II. with its introduction of *The Lady and the Monster* be explained? Why, moreover, should one variant having *The Ransomed Woman* fall into Class II., while three others fall into Class I.? Such an assumption, it is clear, would be self-destructive.

The only alternative is to suppose that *The Water of Life* entered into combination with simple or compound types of *The Grateful Dead* at more than one time and in more than one region. That *The Grateful Dead* united with *The Poison Maiden* and *The Ransomed Woman* rather early and quite independently abundant evidence goes to show; that *The Water of Life* is an independent motive and that, like at least two of the other themes, it was of Asiatic origin has likewise been made clear; that the latter could not have united with *The Grateful Dead* so early as did *The Poison Maiden* and *The Ransomed Woman* is proved by the discrepancies noted above. If it be assumed, on the contrary, that after the compounds *The Grateful Dead* + *The Poison Maiden* and *The Ransomed Woman* had arisen, both they and the simple theme in one or another form came into connection with one or another

[1] P. 143.

form of *The Water of Life* our difficulties are in great measure resolved.

With this in mind let us consider the three categories. Sometime before the fourteenth century[1] *The Water of Life*, perhaps in a rather peculiar form, came into contact with *The Grateful Dead*, both simple and combined with *The Ransomed Woman*,[2] in eastern or central Europe. With each form it seems to have united, giving rise in the century named to the German romance of *Treu Heinrich* and the legend of Nicholas by Gobius, as well as, sooner or later, to the folk-tales with which it has been found combined in those regions within the past hundred years. The territorial limitation of the resulting type is a point in the favour of the proposed theory, though I cannot but be aware that this may be disturbed by a variant outside the seemingly fixed circle. Yet even so, the relation of the variants of Class I. to the themes concerned appears to be pretty definitely established. With Class III. the matter is even simpler. According to my view, some form of *The Grateful Dead*, more or less confused with one of the countless versions of *The Thankful Beasts* met with a very clear type of *The Water of Life* in southern or south-western Europe by or before the thirteenth century.[3] With this it united and gave rise to an Old French romance (later turned into Dutch) and to a considerable body of folk-tales, which have not strayed far from the point of departure save in one instance,[4] where the means of transmission is not difficult to ascertain. Apparently the thankful beast was not absolutely in solution, since in *Maltese* and *Venetian* the human ghost resumes its characteristic rôle.[5] With Class

---

[1] The date of *Treu Heinrich*. This gives the date *a quo*.

[2] The compound existed before the fourteenth century certainly. See pp. 117 f.

[3] The date is here determined by the existence of *Walewein*.   [4] *Brazilian*.

[5] *Venetian* has, however, united with other material, which may account for this in the one case.

II. the case is different and more difficult of explanation. Here the compound has no definite territorial limits, and it is besides of a very complicated character. We have to suppose that *The Lady and the Monster*, a *märchen* allied to *The Water of Life*, was afloat in Europe somewhat before the early sixteenth century.[1] There it met and united with *The Grateful Dead*, in its simple form on the one hand, giving rise to three of our variants, and on the other hand separately with the compounds having *The Poison Maiden* and *The Ransomed Woman*. The former double compound must have been made fairly early,[2] since it has been found in such widely separated countries as Rumania and Ireland, and furnished one of the most important elements to the making of a sixteenth century English play, Peele's *Old Wives' Tale*. The second of the double compounds is unfortunately represented on our list by a single folk-tale only, and may possibly be a later formation.

Such, then, seems to be the relationship of *The Water of Life* and allied motives to the main theme of our study,—purely subsidiary and relatively late. The theory which has been proposed involves the necessity of placing the entrance of the Semitic *märchen* into Europe not much earlier than the twelfth century, though such matters of chronology must be left somewhat to speculation; it shows the points of contact between the various motives concerned; and it avoids contradictions of space and time. Writer and reader may perhaps congratulate themselves on finding so clear a road through the maze. Should subsequent discovery of material necessitate modification of the views here expressed, it should be welcomed by both with equal pleasure.

[1] The date of Straparola, one of whose stories belongs to this class.

[2] The compound *The Grateful Dead + The Poison Maiden* had been in existence since the end of the first century, as *Tobit* proves.

CHAPTER VII.

THE RELATIONS OF *THE GRATEFUL DEAD* TO *THE SPENDTHRIFT KNIGHT*, *THE TWO FRIENDS*, AND *THE THANKFUL BEASTS*.

WE have met at various points in our study with tales in which the motive of the hero's fateful journey was his impoverishment through extravagance; we have seen that many variants make the division of a child part of the agreement between the ghost and the hero; and we have noted the appearance of the ghost in the form of a beast in a large number of instances. The bearing of these phenomena we shall do well to investigate before proceeding to general conclusions. Occurring as they do in versions which have been assigned on other accounts to different categories, are they of sufficient importance to disturb the classification already proposed? Furthermore, what cause can be found for their introduction? Are they in reality sporadic, or are they the result of some determinable factor in the history of the cycle?

Eleven variants, namely, *Richars, Oliver, Lope de Vega, Dianese, Old Swedish, Icelandic I., Icelandic II., Ritter-triuwe, Treu Heinrich,* and *Sir Amadas,* have more or less clearly expressed the motive of a knight who has exhausted his patrimony and goes out to recruit his fortunes by winning a princess in a tourney. The figure of such a knight or adventurer is not an uncommon one in the fiction of Europe, and scarcely requires illustration. Of the variants just named all except *Oliver*, *Lope de Vega*, and *Old Swedish* actually state that the hero sets out from home on account of his poverty. In the two former the motive of the incestuous step-mother is introduced in place of this, and in *Old Swedish* the trait is obscured without any substitution, implying that the hero is led merely by ambition to undertake the tourney. On the other hand, the tourney occurs in all save *Icelandic I.* and *II.*, which are the only folk-tales in the list. The second of these, more-over, makes the hero a merchant instead of a knight; but since the two come from the same island and are in other respects rather similar,[1] this is perhaps not very significant.

Looking at the matter from another point of view, we find that *Richars*, *Lion de Bourges*, *Dianese*, *Old Swedish*, *Rittertriuwe*, and *Sir Amadas* form a group by themselves,[2] and are uncompounded with any one of the themes with which *The Grateful Dead* is most frequently allied. *Oliver* and *Lope de Vega* are treated under the compound with *The Ransomed Woman*, where on account of the rescue of the hero by the ghost they probably belong;[3] and *Icelandic I.* and *II.* are clearly of that type. *Treu Heinrich*[4] shows the combination of the central theme with *The Water of Life*, and can in the nature of the case have no direct connection with the other romance stories under consideration, even though it belongs to a class in which *The Ransomed Woman* sometimes appears.[5] In view of these discrepancies of position with reference to compounds which are clearly established, we are certainly not justified in assuming that *The Spendthrift Knight* has had anything more than a superficial relationship to *The Grateful Dead*. To make it a basis of classification or to attach any

[1] See pp. 89 f.   [2] See pp. 33-40.   [3] See pp. 92-96.
[4] See pp. 131-134.   [5] P. 149.

considerable weight to its appearance here and there would be contrary to the only safe method of procedure, which is to follow the evidence of events in sequence rather than isolated traits. The very fact that none of the compounds with *The Poison Maiden* contains any such motive as this of the knight and the tourney shows that it must be comparatively late and really an interloper in the family.

As to the way by which it entered the cycle, one must conclude that it was afloat in Europe before the thirteenth century,[1] and furnished a very natural opening for a tale in which a youth goes into the world to seek adventure or profit. Were a lady to be won by the help of the ghost, it would magnify the hero's part, if he were given an opportunity to take some very direct share in the wooing. So in the group of which *Richars* and *Sir Amadas* are members the new theme supplied the means of winning a lady, which would otherwise be lacking. In *Oliver* and *Lope de Vega* it has perhaps supplanted the ransom of a maiden, which is the trait to be expected, if they are rightly placed among the variants of the type *The Grateful Dead + The Ransomed Woman*. It will be noted that in the two Icelandic tales, which conform closely to the type, the tourney does not appear. There seems to be reason, therefore, for supposing that the new material touched our central theme at least twice, combining with the prototype of the *Amadas* group and of the Icelandic folk-stories. The authors of *Oliver* and *Treu Heinrich* may have adopted it consciously, and so these variants should be left out of account.

Before leaving the matter, however, it must be noted that in *Tobit* the hero leaves home on account of the poverty of his father to seek the help of a relative. The ever-recurring possibility of a recollection of *Tobit*

[1] The date of *Richars*.

on the part of the European story-tellers[1] should not be forgotten. To argue that the suggestion of adapting *The Spendthrift Knight* was due to a conscious or unconscious recollection of the Apocrypha would be laying too much stress upon what can at best be nothing more than conjecture, but there can be no harm in the surmise that such may have been the case.

The matter of the division of his child or children by the hero to fulfil the bargain made with his helper must next be discussed. This occurs in twenty-five of the variants which we have considered, namely: *Lithuanian II., Transylvanian, Lope de Vega, Oliver, Jean de Calais I.-X., Basque II., Gaelic, Irish I., Breton I., III.,* and *VII., Simrock I., II.,* and *VIII., Sir Amadas,* and *Factor's Garland.* With reference to one group where the trait appears[2] I have already spoken at some length of *The Two Friends,* and I have referred to the introduction of the children as they have appeared in scattered variants. I now wish to call the reader's attention to the general aspects of the question. What relation has the use of this trait in versions of *The Grateful Dead* to the theme which I call *The Two Friends*?

It must first be noted that the motive as it appears in *Amis and Amiloun* requires[3] that the hero slay his children for the healing of his foster-brother and sworn friend. Now of the twenty-five variants of *The Grateful Dead* just named only *Oliver* and *Lope de Vega* have this factor,—the others merely state that the helper asked the hero to fulfil his bargain by giving up his only child,[4] or giving up one of his two children,[5] or dividing his only child,[6] or dividing his three children.[7]

[1] See pp. 50, 58.   [2] See pp. 92-111.   [3] See p. 92.

[4] As in *Lithuanian II., Breton VII., Simrock I.,* and *Factor's Garland.*

[5] As in *Transylvanian.*

[6] As in *Jean de Calais I.-X., Basque II., Irish I., Breton I.* and *III., Simrock II.* and *VIII.,* and *Sir Amadas.*

[7] As in *Gaelic.*

The query at once suggests itself as to whether the simple division of the child or children as part of the hero's possessions gave rise to the introduction of the whole theme of *The Two Friends* in *Oliver* and *Lope de Vega*, or whether the twenty-two folk-tales have merely an echo of the theme as there found. To put the question is almost equivalent to answering it. One sees at once that the former is the case. *Lope de Vega* derives directly from *Oliver*,[1] and to the author of that romance must be due the combination of the two themes there presented. Reference to the earlier discussion of the variant[2] will show that he was a conscious adapter of his material.

Yet it by no means follows that the suggestion for the combination was not present in the version of *The Grateful Dead*, which was used in making *Oliver*. Indeed, it seems probable that this source or prototype had the division of the child in somewhat the form in which it appears in so many tales. That such was the case is likely from the fact that of the twenty-two folk variants which refer to the child all but two are of the type *The Grateful Dead + The Ransomed Woman*, to which *Oliver* is approximated. Considering the alterations which the theme was likely to suffer at the hands of a writer who was more or less consciously combining various material in a romance, the wonder is that the type was not more changed than it seems to have been. In point of fact, the position of *Oliver* and its literary successors as examples of the compound comes out more clearly[3] through this examination of their relationship to *The Two Friends*.

As to the introduction of the child, the trait by means of which, according to my theory, the actual combination of motives came about, the two folk-tales of the type *The Grateful Dead + The Poison Maiden* as well as *Sir*

[1] See p. 95. [2] See pp. 93 f. [3] See p. 94.

Amadas, are of great importance. Since the great majority of the variants which have the child belong clearly to the compound type with *The Ransomed Woman*, it is only by reference to these three that one can say with assurance that the modified trait indicates no vital connection with *The Two Friends*. Yet with these in mind there can be little doubt about the matter. The story-tellers have simply extended the division of the hero's possessions from property and wife to child, a process perhaps made easier by the existence of such stories as *The Child Vowed to the Devil*[1] and some forms of the *Souhaits Saint Martin*.[2] This might have happened to any particular variant with equal facility. At the same time, the fact that the change was made in only three cases outside the group, which has *The Ransomed Woman* in combination, gives that family additional solidarity.

In *Oliver, Lope de Vega*, and *Sir Amadas* the motive of *The Spendthrift Knight* appears together with the change or combination just referred to. At first sight, it might appear that there was some essential connection between these two elements foreign to the main theme. Such does not seem to be the case, however, when the matter is further considered. At any rate, I am unable to discover any such link, and am inclined to ascribe the simultaneous appearance of these two factors to chance pure and simple. Neither one is more than a rather late and comparatively unimportant phenomenon as far as *The Grateful Dead* is concerned.

Not infrequently in the course of this study attention has been called to the substitution of a beast for the helping friend of the hero, and in a few cases to the transference of the ghost's entire rôle to an animal. While considering matters of greater importance, it

---

[1] See references in *Publ. Mod. Lang. Ass.* xx. 545.

[2] See my article in *Publ. Mod. Lang. Ass.* xix. 427, 430-432.

seemed best to ignore this in order to avoid unnecessary confusion. The matter is of considerable importance, however, and must here be considered. The question that concerns us is whether the appearance of the beast is of any real moment in the development of the theme.

It is sufficiently clear that the well-known stories of grateful animals and ungrateful men, which were first traced by Benfey,[1] have general outlines different from that of *The Grateful Dead.* Benfey's contention, however, that "konnte der Gedanke von der Dankbarkeit der Thiere schon tief genug auch im Occident einwurzeln, um auch in andere Märchen einzudringen und vielleicht selbst sich in Bildung von verwandten zur Anschauung zu bringen"[2] should be kept in mind. This statement is truer than his later remark[3] that fairies and other superhuman creations of fancy are substituted for animals, instancing our theme as such a case. To argue relationship from the entrance of either helpful beasts, fairies, or ghosts would be dangerous unless the stories in question had the same motive, since they are so frequently found in folk-literature. Indeed, as I have already remarked,[4] one is scarcely called upon to explain the intrusion of thankful or helpful animals at any given point, in view of the fact that the device is almost universally known. Yet if it does not require justification, it may well be of service in the grouping of particular variants.

It is certainly worthy of notice that in eighteen forms of *The Grateful Dead* a beast appears. That these are of several different compound types would show, if it were not clear from what has been said above, that the appearance of an animal furnishes of itself no evidence of any actual amalgamation of narrative themes. It is rather a case where one stock figure of imagination's realm is substituted for another. The better-known character is perhaps more likely to replace the less-known

[1] *Pantschatantra*, i. §71.   [2] i. 207.   [3] i. 219.   [4] Pp. 126 f.

than *vice versa*, but the latter event may happen if the obscurer figure will serve to enliven the tale.

Of the twenty variants in our cycle which have a thankful beast, *Jewish* has the simple theme; *Servian IV.* the combination with *The Poison Maiden; Jean de Calais II., VII.,* and *X., Simrock II., III., V.,* and *VIII.,* and *Oldenburgian* the combination with *The Ransomed Woman;* and *Walewein, Lotharingian, Tuscan, Brazilian, Basque I., Breton IV., V.,* and *VI.,* and *Simrock IX.* the combination with *The Water of Life.*

Now in Jewish [1] the hero is saved from shipwreck [2] by a stone, carried home by an eagle, and there met by a white-clad man, who explains the earlier appearances. This is mere reinforcement of the tale by triplication, and implies nothing more than a certain vigour of imagination on the part of the story-teller. In *Servian IV.,* [3] where the hero spares a fish which he has caught, there appears, on the contrary, to be actual combination with *The Thankful Beasts* as a motive. The fish comes on the scene in human form, and fulfils the part of the grateful dead till the very end, when it leaps back into its element. As for the variants of the compound type with *The Ransomed Woman* there is considerable diversity, yet all of them have merely substitution, not combination. So in *Jean de Calais II., VII.* and *X.,* [4] which are closely allied with other members of the group so named, the beast appears, but in one case as a white bird, in the second as a fox, and in the third as a crow. That this is anything more than a substitution due to the story-teller's individuality cannot be admitted, though knowledge of *The Thankful Beasts* as a motive is not barred out. *Simrock II.* and *VIII.* [5] are likewise nearly related to one another and to *Jean de*

---

[1] See p. 27.

[2] So in *Polish* of the type *The Grateful Dead + The Water of Life* the ghost appears as a plank. See p. 128.

[3] See p. 57.   [4] See pp. 100-102, 104 f.   [5] See pp. 108 ff.

Calais, and they have the same adventitious substitution. *Simrock V.* and *Oldenburgian* are a similar pair,[1] while *Simrock III.*,[2] which is otherwise allied to *Bohemian*, cannot be shown to have any vital connection with *The Thankful Beasts* as a motive. Of all these tales it can be said that they show some influence from such a theme without actual combination. Finally, all the variants of the type *The Grateful Dead + The Water of Life*, which have the animal substituted,[3] belong to a well-defined and centralized group[4] which has had independent existence for centuries. Here the entrance of the beast is of considerable importance to the classification and development of the theme.

Of the part which *The Thankful Beasts* as a motive has played in connection with *The Grateful Dead* it must be said that, on the whole, it has been of very secondary importance. It illustrates, as do *The Spendthrift Knight* and *The Two Friends*, how one current theme may touch and even influence another at several different points without becoming embodied with it. This trait or that may be absorbed as the motives meet, yet the two waves may go their way without mingling.

[1] See pp. 115 f.   [2] See pp. 112 f.
[3] See pp. 135 ff.   [4] See also p. 151.

CHAPTER VIII.

CONCLUSION.

In considering the general development and relations of *The Grateful Dead*, to which we must now turn, it is proper to inquire first of all as to its origin. Hitherto the existence of the story-theme as such has been taken well nigh for granted, though the discussion of variants in simple form necessitated some reference[1] to the point of separation between the *märchen* and whatever beliefs or social customs lie beyond. Now that the tale has been followed through its various modifications and has been proved by a systematic study of its forms to be, if I may use the expression, a living organism, the debateable land outside can be entered with measurable security.

There can be no doubt that *The Grateful Dead* as a theme is based upon beliefs about the sacred duty of burial and upon the customs incident to withholding burial for the sake of revenge or recompense. To study these phenomena in detail is not necessary to the scheme of this book, but belongs rather to the province of primitive religion and law. It is sufficient for our purpose to show the nature and extent of such observances and beliefs for the sake of the light which they may throw on the genesis of the tale itself.

The belief that no obligation is more binding on man than that he pay proper respect to the dead is as old as civilization itself. Indeed, it probably antedates what

[1] See pp. 28 f.

we ordinarily call civilization, since otherwise it could not well be found so widely distributed over the earth in historical times. It evidently rests upon the notion that the soul, when separated from the body, could find no repose.[1] Herodotus tells[2] of the Egyptian law, which permitted a man to give his father's body in pledge, with the proviso that if he failed to repay the loan neither he nor any of his kin could be buried at all. The story, also related by Herodotus,[3] of Rampsinit and the thief, which turns on the latter's successful attempt to rescue his brother's body, illustrates again the value that the Egyptians set upon burial. Their notion seems to have been that the more honour paid the dead, the more bearable would be their lot, though it was regarded as unenviable at best.[4] Among the Magi of Persia, though both burial and burning were prohibited because of the sanctity of earth and fire, the bodies of the dead were cared for according to the strictest of codes, being left to the sun and air on elevated structures.[5] In India the *Rig-Veda*[6] bears witness to similar carefulness in the performance of this sacred duty.

In classical times belief in the necessity of proper burial was widespread. Patroclus, it will be remembered, appears to his friend Achilles, and admonishes him that he should not neglect the dead, at the same time giving a dire picture of the state of the unburied.[7] Pausanias speaks[8] of the conduct of Lysander as reprehensible in not burying the bodies of Philocles and the four thousand slain at Aegospotami, saying that the Athenians did as

---

[1] See the comment of von der Leyen, *Arch. f. d. St. d. n. Spr.* cxiv. 12.

[2] ii. 136.

[3] ii. 121. The story, however, belongs to the domain of general literature.

[4] See A. Wiedemann, *Die Toten und ihre Reiche im Glauben der alten Aegypter*, p. 21 (*Der alte Orient*, ii, 1900).

[5] *Zend-Avesta*, Vendîdâd, chaps. v.-xii.   [6] x. 18. 1.

[7] *Iliad*, xxiii. 71 ff.   [8] ix. 32.

much for the Medes after Marathon, and even Xerxes for the Lacedaemonians after Thermopylae. The story told by Cicero[1] of Simonides gives definite proof of the concrete nature of the reverential feeling among both Greeks and Romans. Suetonius in his life of Caligula relates that when the emperor's body was left half burned and unburied, ghosts filled the palace and garden.

An example of the mediaeval belief is found in the Middle High German *Kudrun*, written at the end of the twelfth century or the beginning of the thirteenth.

> "Daz hâst wol gerâten," sprach der von Sturmlant.
> "jâ sol man verkoufen ir ros und ir gewant,
> die dâ ligent tôte, daz man der armen diete
> nâch ir lîbes ende von ir guote disen frumen biete."
>
> Dô sprach der degen Îrolt: "sol man ouch die begraben,
> die uns den schaden tâten, od sol man si die raben
> und die wilden wolve ûf dem wérde lâzen niezen?"
> dô rieten daz die wîsen, daz sie der einen ligen niht enliezen.[2]

The *Annamite* tale cited in the third chapter[3] and *Servian VI.*, likewise summarized in connection with variants having the story-theme in simple form,[4] bear witness to the effect that the widespread belief has had upon folk-tales now in circulation. The connection of these two tales with the *märchen* as such is so vague that they serve the end of illustrating its growth from popular belief rather than the relationship of one form to another. So also the story from Brittany, printed by Sébillot,[5] which tells how a ghost came to workmen in a mill demanding Christian interment for its body then buried under the foundations, serves the same end, though no reward is mentioned. Sometimes the neglect of burial by a person brings unpleasant results to him, as is witnessed by a tale from Guernsey.[6] A fisherman neg-

---

[1] See pp. 26 f.
[2] Ed. Bartsch, xviii. st. 910 and 911.   [3] P. 27.   [4] P. 28.
[5] *Traditions et superstitions de la Haute-Bretagne*, 1882, i. 238 f.
[6] MacCulloch, *Guernsey Folk Lore*, 1903, pp. 283 f.

lected to bury a body which he encountered on the coast, and, when he reached his home, found the ghost awaiting him. An Indian tale illustrates the belief that the dead become vampires when funeral rites are not performed.[1]

In most versions of *The Grateful Dead* a corpse is left unburied either because creditors remain unpaid or the surviving relatives cannot pay for Christian burial. From sixteenth century Scotland we have evidence that the latter trait is based on actual custom. Sir David Lyndesaye, in *The Monarche*, while describing the ex- actions of the clergy, says:

> Quhen he hes all, than, vnder his cure,
> And Father and Mother boith ar dede,
> Beg mon the babis, without remede:
> They hauld the Corps at the kirk style;
> And thare it moste remane ane quhyle,
> Tyll thay gett sufficient souerte
> For thare kirk rycht and dewite.[2]

This evidence for the widespread belief in the pious duty of burial and for the custom of withholding burial in cases where the dead man was poor, though it might easily be increased in bulk, makes very clear at least two matters. The tale of *The Grateful Dead* might have arisen almost anywhere and in almost any age since the time of the Egyptians. Again, when once it had been formed, it was likely to be reinforced or changed by the beliefs and customs prevalent in the lands to which it came.

The first matter at once suggests the question as to whether, after all, the *märchen* has not been more than once discovered by the imagination of story-tellers,— whether it has not sprung up again and again in dif- ferent parts of the world like different botanical species,

---

[1] See W. Crooke in *Folk-Lore*, xiii. 280-283.

[2] Book iii. vv. 4726 ff. of the whole poem (2nd ed. J. Small, 1883, E. E. T. S. orig. ser. 11, p. 153).

instead of being a single plant which has propagated itself through many centuries. In spite of the evident possibility that such sporadic development might have taken place, I cannot believe that it happened so. If we had to do with some vaguely outlined myth in which only the underlying idea was the same in the several groups of variants, and if this vague tale were narrated among peoples of absolutely no kinship to one another, say by the Indians of North America and the Zulus, one could have no reasonable doubt that similar conditions had produced similar tales. Such stories exist in numbers sufficient to render untenable the old hypothesis of Oriental origins in anything like the form in which it was held by Benfey or even Cosquin.

In cases like that of *The Grateful Dead*, however, the matter is entirely different. The theme is comparatively a complicated one, and it is found only in lands whose inhabitants are connected either by blood or by social and political intercourse.[1] It has preserved its integrity for nearly a score of centuries, though suffering many changes of details, and a variety of combinations with other themes. To my mind such an involved relationship as that worked out in the preceding chapters proves conclusively that the story is one, that the connection between variants is more than fortuitous. Inductive logic makes the belief inevitable. Any other theory would involve us in a bewildering net of contradictions, from which escape could be found only in the avowal that nothing whatever can be known about narrative development.

If the seemingly inevitable conclusion be accepted that *The Grateful Dead* is an organism with a life history of its own, the question at once suggests itself as to when and where it came into being. As to its

---

[1] *Annamite* is an exception, but it cannot be regarded as having any organic connection with the cycle.

ultimate origin, however, only a very imperfect answer can be given. Surmise and theory are all that can aid us here. Liebrecht was of the opinion that the story was of European rather than Oriental origin,[1] even though he did not accept Simrock's theory that it was Germanic. Notwithstanding the fact that most variants are European, this hypothesis seems to me very improbable. *Tobit*, the earliest variant which we possess,[2] is distinctly Semitic in origin and colouring. Other versions from Asia, like *Jewish*, *Armenian*, and *Siberian*, though modern folk-tales, add weight to the evidence of the apocryphal story, especially since the one last named comes from a somewhat remote region where European narratives could not without difficulty have much direct influence. Of course it is possible to suppose that the theme came to the Semites from the West, and was by them disseminated in Asia;[3] but the early date of *Tobit* renders it unlikely that such was the case. Certainly it is more reasonable from the evidence at hand to believe in the Oriental origin of the *märchen*. As to the particular region of Asia where it was probably first related, nothing can be said with security. Yet since there is no evidence that it has ever been known in India, Western Asia, and perhaps the region inhabited by the Semites, may be considered, at least tentatively, its first home.

The age of the theme cannot definitely be measured. It is possible, however, to say that it must have existed at least as early as the beginning of our era. *Tobit* is of assistance again here. As the book is believed to have been written during the reign of Hadrian (76-138 A.D.) and as it has the motive in a compound form, which is unlikely to have arisen immediately after the

---

[1] See *Heidelberger Jahrbücher*, 1868, p. 449.

[2] Ruling out *Simonides*, of course, as not clearly belonging to the cycle.

[3] *Siberian*, it will be remembered, is of the same type as *Tobit*.

simple story was first set afloat, there is little danger of over-statement in saying that the latter must have been known at least as early as the first part of first century A.D., or more probably before the birth of Christ. Any statement beyond this would rest on idle speculation.

After *The Grateful Dead* was once established as a narrative, its development can be traced with some degree of precision, though not without many gaps here and there. Its history is largely a matter of combinations with originally independent themes, with an occasional landmark in the form of a literary version. The most notable compounds into which it has entered are those with *The Poison Maiden, The Ransomed Woman,* and certain types connected with *The Water of Life.* That it entered into other minor compounds at various stages gives evidence that it retained its independence long after the first union took place, even though examples of the simple type are so hard to find and in some cases of such doubtful character.

Probably the first combination of the theme was with *The Poison Maiden,* which the valuable evidence of *Tobit* enables us to date as taking place as early as the middle of the first century and in western Asia. *The Poison Maiden* probably came originally from India by way of Persia,[1] and was certainly widely distributed. Among the Semites it would naturally first meet any tale which had other than Indian origin, so that the existence of *Tobit* at so early a date is only what one would expect, looking at the matter in this retrospective fashion. The amalgamation of these two themes, when once they had come into the same region, was natural. They had the necessary point of contact in the treatment of the hero's wife by a helpful friend, who played an important part in each. In *The Poison Maiden* she

[1] See Hertz, pp. 151-155.

received short shrift, being possessed of a poisonous glance or bite, or of snakes ready to destroy the man who married her.[1] In *The Grateful Dead* she was innocent, but had to be divided to satisfy the claims of a being who had helped her husband.[2] The part of the friend was less well motivated in *The Poison Maiden* than in *The Grateful Dead*, so that it was natural for the themes to unite at a common point and produce a compound at once more complete and more thrilling than were the simpler forms. This combination must have been made not by a conscious literary worker, for, had it been, *Tobit* would surely stand less independent of the later versions than is actually the case, but by the tellers of folk-tales, in a manner quite unconscious and altogether unstudied. The stories combined of themselves, so to say.

From Semitic lands, if it was indeed there made, the compound seems to have travelled into Europe as well as into other parts of Asia.[3] It has spread during the intervening centuries throughout the length and breadth of Europe, always remaining a genuinely popular tale. As far as my knowledge goes, it did not appear in literature from the time when the Hebrew book of *Tobit* was written till Peele's *Old Wives' Tale* was presented some fifteen centuries later on the English stage. In the nineteenth century it again appeared to the reading public in the version which the Dane Andersen made from a Norse folk-tale. Yet the story in all versions of the compound extant is unmistakably the same, though it has suffered more changes in detail than would be worth while to enumerate here,

---

[1] For examples, see Hertz, pp. 106-115.

[2] It is not clear whether she was actually divided in the primitive forms, or merely threatened. In either case the union would take place as stated.

[3] *Armenian* and *Siberian* give adequate evidence as to the truth of the latter statement, though more Asiatic variants of this type are to be desired.

since they have already been noted in the chapter dealing with the type. The most important modification
which it sustained was due to its meeting *The Lady
and the Monster* and absorbing elements of that tale.
How early this took place it is impossible to say, since
George Peele's play is the only literary monument that
helps to fix any date. A considerable stretch of time
must, however, be allowed for the passage of a folk-
tale from the extreme east of Europe to England.
That the secondary combination was indeed made in
eastern Europe admits of definite proof. All the known
variants of *The Grateful Dead + The Poison Maiden*
from the west have *The Lady and the Monster* as well,
while three Slavic east-European versions[1] are of this
type. It follows that the compound must have been
formed in the east and carried to the west, since otherwise the distribution should be precisely the opposite
of that which obtains. Moreover, had the compound
been made in Asia, it is improbable that it would have
left such a comparatively feeble trace in the eastern
part of the continent of Europe and later have conquered
all the west. Other combinations, primary and secondary,
have also arisen; but, if the collection of variants hitherto
made is at all adequate, they are of inconsiderable
importance.

Meanwhile, the simple theme of *The Grateful Dead*
passed into Europe by other paths. Once over the
border, it met a tale with which it readily combined,
producing a type not less influential than the one just
mentioned. This new motive was *The Ransomed Woman*,
the origin of which is at present quite unknown. Though
it is seemingly Oriental in character, all versions yet
unearthed come from Europe, so that its *provenance* must
be left in uncertainty. At all events, it was known in
eastern Europe, and it was there in all probability that

[1] *Servian III.*, *Esthonian II.*, and *Rumanian I.*

it became amalgamated with *The Grateful Dead.* How early this took place cannot be stated, but long enough before the fourteenth century to allow the passage of the compound type to France by that time, when it was retold by Gobius with a good deal of mutilation in his *Scala Celi.*[1] The points of contact, which led to the combination, have already been discussed in the chapter dealing with the type.[2] Suffice it to say at this point that they were, in brief, the journey of the hero, his rescue, and the wife whom he gained at the end of the story. As in the case of *The Poison Maiden,* the compound seems to have arisen quite naturally by means of these correspondences, with the end of making a more romantic and satisfactory tale. That it took place quite unconsciously seems clear, but that the result was successful is proved by the solidarity of the type thus produced, though it has subsequently been carried into every part of Europe. The relationship of versions, between thirty and forty in number, is unmistakable.

That the simple motive of *The Grateful Dead* was not exhausted by the two remarkable combinations just treated, that it retained its individuality and independence, is shown by the various minor combinations discussed in the third chapter. It is altogether probable that other examples of such simple compounds as those containing *The Swan-Maiden, Puss in Boots,* and a story like that told of Pope Gregory[3] are in existence, and may be found by later study. One can speak only with reference to material at command. Very likely other combinations than those treated here are in existence and may also appear, either in sporadic cases or in groups. But, the reader may ask, if the motive is found in so many compounds, both with and without *The Poison Maiden* and *The Ransomed Woman,* why does it not occur

---

[1] See p. 82.   [2] See pp. 116 f.
[3] See pp. 40 f.

more frequently, at least in folk-literature, without combination ? To this I should reply that the story is an ancient one, which has many points of correspondence with other themes. By reason of these traits it has absorbed, or has been absorbed by, these other tales, until now it is difficult to find examples of the simple form. A thousand years ago, or some such matter, they may, indeed, have been frequently retold by the firesides of Europe, though now they are practically unknown. The constant tendency of folk-tales to change from simplicity to complexity would in time cause the pure theme to be generally forgotten. Nevertheless, its existence could be proved, even though no example still remained, for the various independent compounds would be inexplicable on any other theory. In the case of *The Grateful Dead*, the tales, to which it has been joined, have been so interwoven with its substance that it is quite impossible to believe, for example, that the combination with *The Ransomed Woman* proceeded from that with *The Poison Maiden*.

But these simple compounds with a single foreign theme do not complete the tale. When once they were formed, they in turn had each a history of its own, with infinite possibilities of absorbing traits from other stories or even entire themes. In the case of the latter, a reason could always be found in such points of contact as I have already mentioned, or so I believe, if the material were sufficient for proper comparison. In this way arose the complicated types treated in chapter six, where the manner of combination is readily seen.[1] Sometimes, it is probable, subtraction has taken place as well as addition, but apparently only when it has not involved the disentangling of various traits. For example, many variants have been noted where one of the two most striking features of our central theme, the burial

[1] See pp. 125-127, 151 f.

of the dead debtor, has disappeared ; yet in every case the rest of the plot has remained unimpaired. The more complicated the variant, the better able is the investigator to place its kinship to other variants, provided that he has the requisite material and the patience to follow up the clues that every such labyrinth affords.

The most striking facts of general import to the study of folk-narrative that have developed in the course of this prolonged consideration of *The Grateful Dead* may be briefly summarized in conclusion. It has been shown once again that the story has an organic life of its own, whether it comes from the East or the West, whether it be founded upon some fact of social custom or belief, or on the imaginings of a moralist of antiquity.[1] Once started, it will go its way through divers lands and ages, yet retain unaltered the essential features of its plot. Call it story-skeleton, or better, living organism, it always keeps its structural integrity, no matter whether told as a pious legend or a *conte à rire*. Of no less importance than this is the fact that whatever serious changes take place in its form are not fortuitous, mere whimsical alterations due to the fancy of story-tellers, but are due to capabilities of expansion or combination in the plot itself. Whenever two themes with points of resemblance or contact come into the same region, they are in the long run pretty certain to unite, each retaining its individuality, but merging in the other. This principle is well illustrated in the history of *The Grateful Dead*. The marriages of stories seem never to be merely for convenience, except in the hands of conscious writers, but to be the result of attraction and real compatibility. That, I take it, is why and how narratives develop.

Were it necessary to justify such studies as the present,

---

[1] See the author's study, "Forerunners, Congeners, and Derivatives of the Eustace Legend " in *Publ. Mod. Lang. Ass.* xix. 335-448.

one might add that, apart from helping to the settlement of such more general questions as those just mentioned, they throw light on the sources of particular literary works better than does the haphazard search for parallels, and they often enable the student to see the relations between the literatures of neighbouring countries more clearly than he would be able to do without the perspective gained by a comparative consideration of a single theme in many lands. In ways like these the author hopes that this history of *The Grateful Dead* may be serviceable.

THE END.

INDEX.

In order to avoid duplication, variants of *The Grateful Dead* are cited according to the names given them in Chapter II., references to which are printed in italics.

University of Illinois Press
1325 South Oak Street
Champaign, IL 61820-6903
www.press.uillinois.edu